my revision notes

WJEC Level 1/2 Vocational Award

HOSPITALITY AND CATERING

Bev Saunder
Yvonne Mackey

HODDER EDUCATION
AN HACHETTE UK COMPANY

Picture credits

p.6 © bartsadowski/stock.adobe.com; p.8 © WavebreakMediaMicro/stock.adobe.com; p.11 © 279photo/stock.adobe.com; p.13 © Peter Jordan/Alamy Stock Photo; p.15 *t* © Jupiterimages/Pixland/Thinkstock, *b* © Andrey Popov/stock.adobe.com; p.17 © auremar/stock.adobe.com; p.18 © Kzenon/stock.adobe.com; p.21 © LoloStock/stock.adobe.com; p.23 *t* © Balint Radu/stock.adobe.com, *b* © RSPCA Assured; p.24 © Antonio_Diaz/iStock/Thinkstock; p.29 © Monkey Business/stock.adobe.com; p.30 © TripAdvisor; p.31 © Gorodenkoff/stock.adobe.com; p.32 © Compass Group; p.33 *t* © Russums.co.uk, *b* © Sam Bailey/Hodder Education; p.34 © pioneer – Fotolia; p.37 © mavoimages/stock.adobe.com; p.38 © Monkey Business/stock.adobe.com; p.40 © WavebreakMediaMicro/stock.adobe.com; p.42 © Jale Ibrak/stock.adobe.com; p.48 © jusep/stock.adobe.com; p.49 © Ammit/stock.adobe.com; p.56 © BSIP SA/Alamy Stock Photo; p.59 © Patti McConville/Alamy Stock Photo; p.60 © dusanpetkovic1/stock.adobe.com; p.61 © Lucky Dragon/stock.adobe.com; p.64 © Russums.co.uk; p.69 © Ingor Normann – Fotolia; p.71 © Andrew Callaghan/Hodder Education; p.74 *t* © tinglee1631/stock.adobe.com, *b* Coeliac UK; p.79 *tl* © mavoimages/stock.adobe.com, *tr* © Ministr-84/Shutterstock.com, *ml* © easaab/stock.adobe.com, *mr* © Jean Vaillancourt/123RF, *b* © v/stock.adobe.com; p.81 *l* © tupungato/123rf.com, *tr* © Lance Bellers/Shutterstock.com, *br* © Imagestate Media (John Foxx)/London V3037; p.87 *l* © Russums.co.uk, *m* © Russums.co.uk, *r* © Compass Group; p.94 © Eric Ferguson - iStockphoto.com; p.95 *t* © Monkey Business/stock.adobe.com, *b* © Patrizia Tilly – Fotolia; p.96 © Vegetarian Society; p.97 © monkeybusinessimages - iStock via Thinkstock/Getty Images; p.101 1st © am13photo/stock.adobe.com, 2nd © leszekglasner/stock.adobe.com, 3rd © artitcom/stock.adobe.com, 4th © Africa Studio/stock.adobe.com, 5th © Sarah Jane – Fotolia, 6th © nerudol/stock.adobe.com, 7th © Andrew Callaghan/Hodder Education; p.103 © lzf - iStock via Thinkstock/Getty Images; p.104 © purtof1/stock.adobe.com; p.108 © Assured Food Standards; p.110 © Crown copyright 2016. Public Health England in association with the Welsh Government, Food Standards Scotland and the Food Standards Agency in Northern Ireland; p.111 © mimagephotos/stock.adobe.com; p.116 *l* © Schlierner – Fotolia, *m* © Difydave - iStock via Thinkstock/Getty Images, *r* © arinahabich- iStock via Thinkstock/Getty Images; p.117 *tl* © Nikodash - iStock via Thinkstock/Getty Images, *tm* © Yeko Photo Studio/stock.adobe.com, *tr* © Andrew Callaghan/Hodder Education, *mr* © Africa Studio/stock.adobe.com, *br* © st-fotograf – Fotolia; p.118 1st © natashaphoto/stock.adobe.com, 2nd © gourmetphotography/stock.adobe.com, 3rd © uaurelijus/Shutterstock.com, 4th © dannyburn/stock.adobe.com, 5th © Maren Winter/stock.adobe.com, 6th © Patryk Kosmider – Fotolia; p.119 © Andrew Callaghan/Hodder Education; p.120 © Alexander Raths - stock.adobe.com; p.121 © Andrew Callaghan/Hodder Education; p.122 © fatmanphotouk/stock.adobe.com; p.123 © Andrew Callaghan/Hodder Education; p.124 © ldprod/stock.adobe.com; p.125 © Sam Bailey/Hodder Education; p.126 © Getty Images/Thinkstock/iStockphoto/Zoonar RF; p.127 *t* © Sam Bailey/Hodder Education, *bl* © Edward Westmacott/stock.adobe.com, *bm* © Ping han/stock.adobe.com, *br* © Dmitriy Syechin/stock.adobe.com; p.128 *t* © Sam Bailey/Hodder Education, *b* © stocksolutions/stock.adobe.com; p.129 © Kristina/stock.adobe.com; p.130 © MELBA PHOTO AGENCY/Alamy Stock Photo; p.131 © ImageShop/Corbis; p.132 © Dream79 - Fotolia.com; p.133 © Andrew Callaghan/Hodder Education; p.135 © Andrew Callaghan/Hodder Education; p.136 © BlueOrange Studio/stock.adobe.com; p.137 © juefraphoto/stock.adobe.com; p.140 *t* © ONYXprj/stock.adobe.com, *b* © ansardi - iStock via Thinkstock/Getty Images; p.141 © Andrew Callaghan/Hodder Education; p.143 © Andrew Callaghan/Hodder Education; p.144 *l* © paulacobleigh/stock.adobe.com, *r* © andesign101/stock.adobe.com; p.145 © Andrew Callaghan/Hodder Education; p.147 © keith morris/Alamy Stock Photo; p.148 © DJC/Alamy Stock Photo

Every effort has been made to trace all copyright holders, but if any have been inadvertently overlooked, the Publishers will be pleased to make the necessary arrangements at the first opportunity.

Although every effort has been made to ensure that website addresses are correct at time of going to press, Hodder Education cannot be held responsible for the content of any website mentioned in this book. It is sometimes possible to find a relocated web page by typing in the address of the home page for a website in the URL window of your browser.

Hachette UK's policy is to use papers that are natural, renewable and recyclable products and made from wood grown in well-managed forests and other controlled sources. The logging and manufacturing processes are expected to conform to the environmental regulations of the country of origin.

Orders: please contact Bookpoint Ltd, 130 Park Drive, Milton Park, Abingdon, Oxon OX14 4SE. Telephone: +44 (0)1235 827827. Fax: +44 (0)1235 400401. Email education@bookpoint.co.uk Lines are open from 9 a.m. to 5 p.m., Monday to Saturday, with a 24-hour message answering service. You can also order through our website: www.hoddereducation.co.uk

ISBN: 978 1 5104 7333 1

© Bev Saunder and Yvonne Mackey 2019

First published in 2019 by
Hodder Education,
An Hachette UK Company
Carmelite House
50 Victoria Embankment
London EC4Y 0DZ
www.hoddereducation.co.uk

Impression number   10   9   8   7   6   5   4
Year   2023   2022   2021   2020

Cover photo © Anton – stock.adobe.com

Illustrations by Aptara Inc.

Typeset in India by Aptara Inc.

Printed in Spain.

A catalogue record for this title is available from the British Library.

Get the most from this book

Everyone has to decide his or her own revision strategy, but it is essential to review your work, learn it and test your understanding. These Revision Notes will help you to do that in a planned way, topic by topic. Use this book as the cornerstone of your revision and don't hesitate to write in it: personalise your notes and check your progress by ticking off each section as you revise.

Tick to track your progress

Use the revision planner on pages 4 and 5 to plan your revision, topic by topic. Tick each box when you have:

● revised and understood a topic

● tested yourself

● practised exam questions and gone online to check your answers and complete the quick quizzes.

You can also keep track of your revision by ticking off each topic heading in the book. You may find it helpful to add your own notes as you work through each topic.

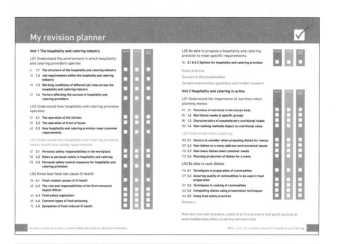

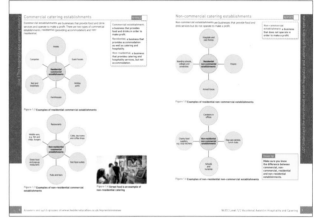

Features to help you succeed

Exam tips

Expert tips are given throughout the book to help you polish your exam technique in order to maximise your chances in the exam.

Typical mistakes

The authors identify the common mistakes candidates make and explain how you can avoid them.

Now test yourself

These short, knowledge-based questions provide the first step in testing your learning. Answers are given online at **www.hoddereducation.co.uk/ myrevisionnotes**

Revision activities

These activities will help you understand each topic in an interactive way.

Definitions and key words

Clear, concise definitions of essential key terms are provided where they first appear.

Exam practice

Practice exam questions are provided on page 84. Use them to consolidate your revision and practise your exam skills.

Online

Go online to check your answers and to try out the extra quick quizzes at **www.hoddereducation.co.uk/ myrevisionnotes**

My revision planner

Unit 1 The hospitality and catering industry

			REVISED	TESTED	EXAM READY

LO1 Understand the environment in which hospitality and catering providers operate

LO2 Understand how hospitality and catering provision operates

LO3 Understand how hospitality and catering provision meets health and safety requirements

LO4 Know how food can cause ill health

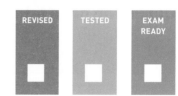
Now test yourself answers, exam practice answers and quick quizzes at www.hoddereducation.co.uk/myrevisionnotes

Unit 1 LO1 Understand the environment in which hospitality and catering providers operate

1.1 The structure of the hospitality and catering industry

The **hospitality** and **catering** industry provides people with accommodation, food and **beverages** outside of the home.

> **Hospitality**: providing accommodation, food and drinks in a variety of places outside the home.
>
> **Catering**: providing food and drinks services to customers.
>
> **Beverage**: a drink other than water.

Types of provider

REVISED

The providers of hospitality and catering can be divided into four groups:

- hotels, campsites and other accommodation
- food services, such as restaurants, pubs, takeaways, cafes, coffee shops, clubs and motorway services
- contract catering for private customers and public sector customers, such as hospitals
- events and conferences.

Types of service

REVISED

There are many different types of food service. The way food is served to the customer will depend on the place where the food is to be eaten.

Table 1.1 Types of food service

Food service	Description
Formal restaurant	Food is usually served to customers by waiting staff: • **plate**: the meal is plated up and brought to the customer's table by waiting staff • **waiting service**: the food is served to customers at the table by waiting staff • **gueridon** (trolley or movable service): the customer's food is cooked at the table, usually for dramatic effect, for example flambéed steaks and crêpes
Street food	Ready-to-eat food or drink sold on the street or in a public place, such as at a market or festival ➡

Figure 1.1 A formal restaurant

Table 1.1 Types of food service (continued)

Food service	Description
Self-service	Customers help themselves to food, for example a carvery; in a carvery the meat is on display and carved by a chef, and the customer can help themselves to vegetables, sauces and gravy
Fast food	Food is made to order very quickly and can be taken away from the restaurant or stall to eat; seats and tables are often provided
Cafeteria	Small or inexpensive restaurant or coffee bar, serving light meals and refreshments
Takeaway	Takeaway restaurants (for example Chinese, Indian and pizzas) take an order and deliver the food to the customer's home; customers can also order at the restaurant and then take the food away to eat it
Buffet	A selection of dishes is laid out for customers to help themselves; different buffet styles include: ● **sit-down buffet**: once the customer has chosen their food from the buffet, they can sit down at a table to eat it ● **stand-up or fork buffet**: once the customer has chosen their food, they stand to eat it; this allows guests to circulate and meet other guests ● **finger buffet**: all the food is prepared to be eaten with the fingers (without the need for a knife and fork); foods are normally bite-size and easy to eat
Automatic vending	Drinks and snacks are stored in a machine with a glass front and items are selected by the customer; they are often coin operated and placed in establishments where it may not always be possible to get access to food, for example colleges and hospitals
Transport catering	A variety of food service options are available on trains, planes and ships
Hotel	Provides overnight accommodation and food and drink options Many hotels offer breakfast, evening meals, bar snacks, lunch and room service (food ordered and delivered to your room); budget hotels usually have a simpler offering
Bed and breakfast	Offers overnight accommodation and breakfast; often these are private family homes where rooms are made available to guests; breakfast is usually served in a dining room or the owner's kitchen

Commercial catering establishments

Commercial establishments are businesses that provide food and drink services and operate to make a profit. There are two types of commercial establishments: **residential** (providing accommodation) and **non-residential**.

Commercial establishment: a business that provides food and drinks in order to make profit.

Residential: a business that provides accommodation as well as catering and hospitality.

Non-residential: a business that provides catering and hospitality services, but not accommodation.

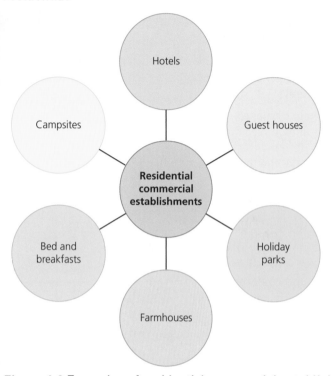

Figure 1.2 **Examples of residential commercial establishments**

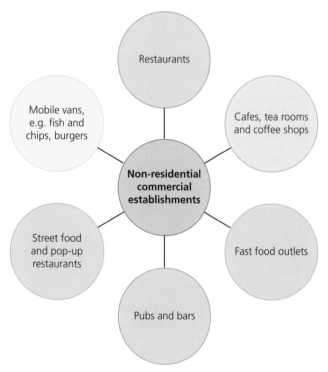

Figure 1.3 **Examples of non-residential commercial establishments**

Figure 1.4 **Street food is an example of non-residential catering**

Answers and quick quizzes at **www.hoddereducation.co.uk/myrevisionnotes**

Non-commercial catering establishments

Non-commercial establishments are businesses that provide food and drink services but do not operate to make a profit.

> **Non-commercial establishment**: a business that does not operate in order to make a profit.

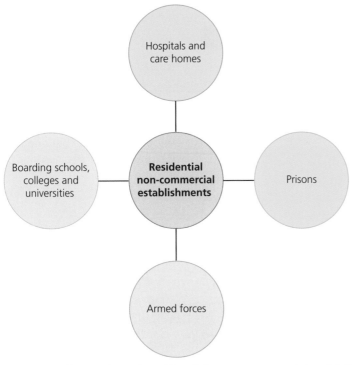

Figure 1.5 Examples of residential non-commercial establishments

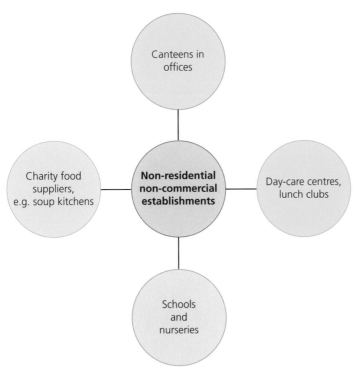

Figure 1.6 Examples of non-residential non-commercial establishments

> **Exam tip**
>
> Make sure you know the difference between commercial, non-commercial, residential and non-residential establishments.

LO1 Understand the environment in which hospitality and catering providers operate

Services provided

REVISED

Commercial and non-commercial residential and non-residential establishments offer different hospitality and catering services.

Table 1.2 Services provided by different types of establishments

Establishment	Services provided	Examples
Commercial residential	Accommodation, housekeeping, food, beverages, conference or training facilities	Hotels, guest houses, campsites, bed and breakfasts, holiday parks, farmhouses
Commercial non-residential	Food and beverages to eat in or take away, areas to sit to eat and drink	Restaurants, cafes, tea rooms, coffee shops, fast food outlets, pubs and bars, street food and pop-up restaurants, mobile vans
Non-commercial residential	Accommodation, food and beverages	Hospitals, care homes, prisons, armed forces, boarding schools, colleges and universities
Non-commercial non-residential	Food and beverages	Canteens in offices, day-care centres, schools and nurseries, charity food suppliers, for example soup kitchens

Suppliers

REVISED

The selection of suppliers is crucial to any establishment. The suppliers used will depend on what food and beverages are sold.

When choosing a supplier, it is important to consider:

● cost of the items required – which supplier is the most competitive and offers the best value for money?
● delivery – how efficient and reliable is it? Do the items arrive in good condition?
● quality of the product – is the quality good enough for what is needed?

The best supplier, at the best price for each product required, can be found by:

● word-of-mouth recommendation
● visiting and checking the supplier's establishment.

Suppliers can be from the:

● primary market – the source of the supply, for example farmers
● secondary market – wholesale from a distributor; this is a company that supplies goods from the source of supply to a retailer or customer, usually in large quantities and at low prices
● tertiary market – retailers or cash-and-carry warehouses.

Figure 1.7 **A food warehouse**

Hospitality at non-catering venues

Some caterers supply food and drinks for functions where catering facilities are not already provided. They are known as **contract caterers**.

- They prepare food for functions such as weddings, banquets and garden parties in private houses.
- They may prepare and cook the food in advance and deliver it to the venue, or they may cook it on site.
- They may also provide staff to serve the food, if required.

Contract caterers are used by a wide range of organisations as it relieves them of the pressures involved in catering for such events.

> **Contract caterer:** caterer supplying food and drinks at a venue where catering facilities are not available.

Hotel and guest house standards

Hotels and guest houses are often given a star rating. Star ratings help customers to know what services and facilities they can expect at a hotel or guest house. The quality of the services provided is rated on a scale from one to five stars.

Table 1.3 Hotel star ratings

Star rating	Requirements to meet this standard
★	At least five bedrooms with en suite facilities
	Open seven days a week
	Guests have access at all times
	Reception area
	Restaurant serving breakfast seven days a week and evening meals five days a week
	Licensed bar
★★	As above plus higher standards of cleanliness, maintenance and hospitality
★★★	Access without a key between 7 a.m. and 11 p.m., access with a key after 11 p.m.
	Dinner served six evenings a week, snacks on the seventh
	Room service for drinks and snacks during the day and evening
	En suite facilities
	Internal telephone system
	Wi-Fi in public areas
★★★★	24-hour room service
	Restaurant open for breakfast and dinner seven days a week
	Wi-Fi in room
	24-hour access and on-duty staff
	En suite facilities
	Enhanced hospitality, for example afternoon tea
	Higher staffing levels
★★★★★	Open all year round
	Proactive service and customer care
	Multilingual receptionists
	Other facilities such as a spa or business centre
	Enhanced services, for example concierge and valet parking
	Restaurant open every day for all meals
	En suite facilities – 80 per cent of rooms have a bath and shower

Food hygiene standards

The Food Standards Agency runs a scheme with local authorities where they score businesses on a scale from zero to five to help customers make an informed choice about where to eat. The rating is usually displayed as a sticker in the window of the premises. The scores mean:

0 Urgent improvement is required

1 Major improvement is necessary

2 Some improvement is necessary

3 Hygiene standards are generally satisfactory

4 Hygiene standards are good

5 Hygiene standards are very good

Figure 1.8 A food hygiene rating sticker

Restaurant standards

The three main restaurant rating systems used in the UK are Michelin stars, AA Rosette Awards and The Good Food Guide reviews.

Michelin stars are a rating system used to grade restaurants on their quality:

- one star is a very good restaurant
- two stars is excellent cooking
- three stars is exceptional cuisine.

AA Rosette Awards score restaurants from one (a good restaurant that stands out from the local competition) to five (cooking that compares with the best in the world).

The Good Food Guide gives restaurants a score from one (capable cooking but some inconsistencies) to ten (perfection).

Environmental standards

The Sustainable Restaurant Association awards restaurants a one-, two- or three-star rating in environmental standards. To achieve this the restaurant has to complete an online survey about sourcing, society and the environment. It is then given an overall percentage for environmental standards:

- one star: 50–59 per cent
- two stars: 60–69 per cent
- three stars: more than 70 per cent.

Job roles within the industry

Management

- The **finance manager** is responsible for the finances and security of the business.
- The **general manager** is responsible for the day-to-day running of the business. It is their responsibility to make a profit and to ensure that staff complete their duties to a high standard. They are also in charge of making sure that good customer service is provided.

Kitchen brigade

- **Head or executive chefs** are in charge of the kitchen. This job involves menu planning, food production, ordering food from suppliers, costing dishes, managing stock, kitchen hygiene, planning staff rotas, and recruiting and training staff. Most head chefs start off as a commis chef before becoming a section chef in charge of a small team of chefs. They need excellent cookery skills, leadership and management skills, budgeting skills, the ability to work under pressure and to meet deadlines, and the ability to keep calm in stressful situations.

- The **sous chef** is directly in charge of food production and often in charge of the day-to-day running of the kitchen. Most sous chefs start off as a commis chef, then become a section chef. They require excellent cookery skills; good organisational skills to manage a busy workload; and excellent communication, teamwork and leadership skills.

- The **chef de partie** (section chef) has responsibility for a particular section of the menu or area of the kitchen, and a varying number of staff to whom they allocate tasks. Jobs carried out vary from one establishment to another depending on the head chef's organisation and size of the establishment. Most large establishments could have chefs de partie in the following areas:
  - sauce chefs
  - pastry chefs – these chefs make breads, pastries, cakes, confectionery, batters, desserts and other baked goods
  - fish chefs
  - roast chefs
  - vegetable chefs
  - soup chefs
  - larder chefs – these chefs prepare cold starters and salads
  - relief chefs – chefs who can be called on if another chef is unable to come to work.

- The **commis chef** or assistant chef does the easier tasks and may be part of an apprenticeship scheme or studying at college. They must enjoy cooking, have good organisational skills, be good communicators and able to work as part of a team.

- The **kitchen porter** washes up and may do basic vegetable preparation.

- The **stock controller** is in charge of all aspects of store keeping and stock control.

All chefs need strong practical skills. The weighing and measuring of ingredients for recipes requires accuracy and consistency, and cooking requires precise timings.

Front of house

- **Receptionists** meet customers and direct them to the correct person or place; they manage visitor lists and booking systems.
- **Waiting staff** prepare tables, give out menus, take orders, serve food and take payment.
- **Bar staff** serve drinks and take food orders, wash up, clear tables, change barrels and fill shelves.
- **Baristas** make and serve hot and cold beverages, in particular different types of coffee such as espressos, cappuccinos and lattes.
- **Sommeliers** give advice on wine choices and describe the taste and aroma of different wines to customers.
- A **concierge** assists hotel guests by making reservations, booking taxis and booking tickets for local attractions and events.

Housekeeping

- The **head housekeeper** allocates jobs to room attendants and ensures that rooms are cleaned correctly. They must communicate well with reception to know what rooms need cleaning, and to inform them once the rooms are ready for the guests.
- **Room attendants** clean and prepare rooms for guests, changing towels and bedding.
- **Maintenance** completes any repairs than can be done in-house and books specialists to carry out particular jobs, such as gas engineers or lift repairs.

Administration

- **Secretaries** help the business to run smoothly by dealing with correspondence, emails, phone calls, filing and ordering.
- **Accountants** do all the bookkeeping and ensure bills and taxes are paid.

> **Revision activity**
>
> Make some revision cards for one of the roles above. Include images and words to help jog your memory. Include information on the role, the work involved, and skills required.

Now test yourself

TESTED ☐

1. Describe the following types of food service.
   - a) Self-service (1 mark)
   - b) Fast food (1 mark)
2. Explain the difference between commercial and non-commercial establishments. (2 marks)
3. When choosing a supplier, what three points should be taken into consideration? (3 marks)
4. Name a skill that would be useful for all front-of-house staff to have. (1 mark)
5. Which of these catering industry roles is an example of a 'front-of-house' role? (1 mark)
   - a) Sous chef
   - b) Sommelier
   - c) Commis chef
   - d) Pastry chef

> **Barista**: makes and serves hot and cold drinks, especially coffee.
>
> **Sommelier**: a specialist wine waiter.

Figure 1.9 A sommelier presents wine

Figure 1.10 A hospitality workforce

> **Typical mistake**
>
> You may be asked to write about the work involved in a particular job. A common mistake is to write very generally. You will gain more marks if you are specific about what each job involves in the hospitality and catering industry.

1.2 Job requirements within the hospitality and catering industry

Supply and demand

- The hospitality industry is the third largest employer in the UK.
- It contributes to 3.2 million jobs through direct employment in the industry and a further 2.8 million jobs indirectly.
- Staffing levels and required skills/job roles might change with demand; supply is affected by the availability of trained staff with the right skills.
- Factors that affect demand are weekday or weekend, the time of year and economic conditions – do people have enough money to spend on eating out/holidays?
- There is a greater demand of staff at seasonal times such as summer and bank holidays, and a greater demand in some parts of the country, for example in tourist destinations.
- Between 2014 and 2017, 65 per cent of job growth has been in restaurants.
- The hospitality and catering industry employs many part-time workers.
- The hospitality industry traditionally employs a young workforce, which means that the shrinking working age population could be a problem in the future. It is estimated that there will be 670,000 fewer 16- to 25-year-olds by 2020.
- As of June 2018, EU nationals make up 40 per cent of the UK's hospitality workforce. Brexit could see a reduction in the number of EU nationals, which could mean that the supply of staff may not meet the demand.
- Outside London, the key cities for growth in the hospitality and catering industry are expected to be Manchester, Liverpool, Edinburgh and Belfast. This is likely to create a range of jobs in those cities.

Jobs for specific needs

Differing customer requirements and trends can lead to the creation of jobs to meet specific needs.

- There is currently growth in the market for vegan, vegetarian and allergen-free dishes. This will present opportunities for smaller restaurants that can be flexible with what they offer.
- Festivals and street food at casual markets are also growing to meet consumer demands.
- The use of technology to order food online (such as Deliveroo, Just Eat and Uber Eats) is increasing.

Rates of pay

Rates of pay in the hospitality and catering industry depend on a worker's age.

- The national minimum wage is the minimum pay per hour workers above school leaving age are entitled to.
- Staff aged 25 and above should get the national living wage, which is higher than the national minimum wage.

- Apprentices are entitled to an apprentice rate if they are under 19, or aged 19 and over and in the first year of their apprenticeship.
- These rates change every April.
- The average salary in the hospitality and catering industry is £25,000 a year. Some average salaries for specific roles are given in Table 1.4.
- Salaries can be affected by supply and demand; for example there is more demand for staff in the holiday season so people may earn more as there may be more shifts available.

Table 1.4 Average salaries in the hospitality and catering industry

Role	Average salary
Hotel management	£37,310
Head executive chef	£36,613
Pastry chef	£30,530
Housekeeper	£24,055
Receptionist	£21,596
Porter	£17,718
Waiting and bar staff	£16,735
Kitchen staff	£16,556

Data from www.reed.co.uk

Training

REVISED

There are many different training courses available to those wanting a career in hospitality and catering. Some examples are provided in Table 1.5.

Table 1.5 Types of training

Level	Type of training
Key Stage 4 school courses	Level 1/2 Vocational Award in Hospitality and Catering
Post 16–19	Colleges offer many courses for those leaving school after Year 11, for example: ● Certificate in Hospitality and Catering Level 1 ● Certificate in Introduction of Culinary Skills Level 1 ● Diploma in Introduction to Professional Cookery Level 1 ● Diploma in Hospitality and Catering Level 2 ● Diploma in Professional Cookery Level 2
Universities	Universities offer degree, HND and HNC courses in subjects such as: ● catering ● hospitality ● culinary arts ● hotel management ● food and beverage service
Apprenticeships	These provide both work experience and training
In-house training	On-the-job training provided by the organisation you work for

Figure 1.11 Training to be a chef

Qualifications and experience

REVISED

- The qualifications you have and the experience you have gained when working in the industry will have an impact on the salary you could earn.
- Executive chefs will have worked their way up through the kitchen brigade. In order to progress in the catering industry, they would need to gain experience as a commis chef, chef for a specific area, such as a pastry chef, chef de partie, sous chef then, finally, executive chef.
- The same applies to front-of-house staff; a room attendant would gain experience to become a housekeeper.
- Apprenticeships and colleges usually require five good GCSE passes, though the entry requirements may be lower for some Level 1 courses. This could be followed by a qualification such as a diploma or certificate.

Personal attributes

REVISED

A **personal attribute** is a quality or a characteristic that a person has. Employers will be looking for a specific set of attributes in their employees.

> **Personal attribute**: a quality or characteristic of a person.

Table 1.6 Personal attributes required for different job roles in the hospitality and catering industry

Job role	Desirable attributes
Waiter/waitress	Attentive listener, good memory, clear communicator, diplomatic, calm and assured, high level of focus and attention, multitasker, can work in a team, physical stamina, courteous and polite, hardworking .
Receptionist	Professional, positive attitude and behaviour, clear communicator, helpful, can work in a team, courteous and polite, can learn skills quickly, calm, composed, approachable
Housekeeper	Physical stamina, tactful, diplomatic, calm, courteous and polite, good memory, can work in a team
Head chef	Organised, able to accept criticism, physical stamina, creative, attention to detail, can handle highly stressful situations, passion for food and cooking
Commis chef	Attentive listener, clear communicator, can work in a team, passion for food and cooking, physical stamina, creative

Figure 1.12 A housekeeper must be diplomatic, courteous and polite, and able to work in a team

Typical mistake

In questions asking about personal attributes, candidates often write about what a person does in their job role, for example: 'a receptionist meets customers and manages bookings'. This does not answer the question. You should instead focus on desirable qualities and characteristics, for example: 'a receptionist should be polite, helpful and a clear communicator'.

Revision activity

Make flash cards for each of the personal attributes given in Table 1.6. On the back of the card write a list of job roles that each of those attributes applies to.

Now test yourself

TESTED

1 Suggest one reason why it may be difficult to recruit staff in the hospitality and catering industry in the future. (1 mark)
2 Explain one area in the hospitality and catering industry that is currently growing. (2 marks)
3 Name two courses available post-16. (2 marks)
4 List four personal attributes that a waiter or waitress should have. (4 marks)
5 List four personal attributes that a head chef should have. (4 marks)

1.3 Working conditions of different job roles across the hospitality and catering industry

Different types of employment contracts

REVISED

A **contract** is a formal document that is designed to protect both the employee and employer. It should explain the duties and responsibilities of the role, rules and procedures, as well as detail working days and hours, pay, holiday entitlement, sickness pay, notice and pension arrangements.

Contract: a formal document outlining the role and responsibilities of a job that is designed to protect both the employee and employer.

Pro rata: proportional/proportionally.

Table 1.7 Different employment contracts

Type of contract	How it works
Full time, permanent	Working days and hours are specified; workers are entitled to sick pay and holiday pay
Part time, permanent	As the above, but reduced sick pay and holiday pay because this is calculated **pro rata** – depending on how many hours are worked
Casual work	This is usually seasonal or covering for a sick colleague; casual workers are entitled to sick pay and holiday pay based on the hours worked
Zero hours	A contract between an employer and a worker in which no minimum hours are given and the worker does not have to accept the work when it is offered; workers are entitled to the minimum wage and holiday pay

Working hours

REVISED

The Working Time Directive states that you can't work longer than 48 hours a week (calculated as an average over 17 weeks). If you are under 18, you can't work more than eight hours a day, or more than 40 hours a week.

Many people in the hospitality and catering industry have to work long and unsociable hours – late nights and at weekends. Chefs may also have to do split shifts, where they work at lunchtime and evenings.

Rates of pay

REVISED

Pay means any money payable to a worker in connection with their employment.

- A **salary** is a form of payment from an employer to an employee, which may be specified in an employment contract. It is a fixed amount per pay period, for example an annual salary.
- A **wage** is money paid by an employer to an employee in exchange for work done. It is usually an hourly rate that is multiplied by the number of hours worked.

Pay can include:

- the hourly/weekly rate agreed with an employer, depending on age, experience and the role and responsibility of the job
- bonus payments, tips, rewards and commission
- sick pay
- holiday pay
- maternity, paternity or adoption pay.

> **Salary**: a fixed payment from an employer to an employee per pay period, for example monthly or annually.
>
> **Wage**: money paid by an employer to an employee in exchange for work done; usually an hourly rate.

Holiday entitlement

Most workers are legally entitled to 28 days (5.6 weeks) of paid holiday a year. An employer can include bank holidays in this allowance.

- Full-time workers who work a five-day week must receive at least 28 days' paid annual leave a year.
- Part-time workers are entitled to a reduced amount of paid holiday depending on the number of days/hours worked. For example, if they work three days a week, they must get at least 16.8 days' leave a year (3×5.6).

Remuneration

Workers in hotels and hospitality can benefit from other remuneration on top of their salary. This can include tips, service charges, subsidised food and accommodation, or bonuses.

- In the UK, restaurant tips are generally between 10 and 20 per cent of the bill; some tips can be higher when excellent service is provided.
- The tips are usually divided out between the staff. This is known as a **tronc** arrangement; the person who works it out and distributes it is called a **troncmaster**.

> **Tronc**: a fund in a hotel or restaurant into which tips and service charges are collected and then shared between staff.
>
> **Troncmaster**: the person who collects and shares money in a tronc arrangement.

- If you pay a service charge when you stay at a hotel or go on a cruise, it will be distributed among the staff members for providing service to the customers.
- Some hotel workers may receive subsidised food and accommodation.
- Bonuses are generally linked to performance. Employers may pay these to workers based on good financial results of a team and/or individual.

Figure 1.13 Leaving a tip

Typical mistake

This is quite a factual section. May sure you learn the key words and definitions thoroughly.

Now test yourself   TESTED

1   List the four types of employment contract.   (4 marks)
2   State how many hours of work you can do each week if you are over 18.   (1 mark)
3   State how many weeks of paid holiday workers are legally entitled to each year.   (1 mark)
4   Explain the term 'tronc arrangement'.   (1 mark)
5   Describe two ways in which workers in hotels and hospitality can be remunerated on top of their salary.   (4 marks)

Revision activity

Make some revision cards on the different types of contract. Include information on who would benefit from each type of contract.

Exam tip

Think about which type of people each different contract of employment would suit – for example, a student or someone with young children.

1.4 Factors affecting the success of hospitality and catering providers

Costs   REVISED

There are three different types of cost:

- **Material costs** – food and drink, consumables such as napkins, cleaning materials and so on.
- **Labour costs** – salaries and wages for all staff connected to the business.
- **Overhead costs** – costs not connected to materials or labour, for example rents, energy, water, telephone, insurance, furniture and furnishings.

Costs can also be divided into:

- **variable costs** – costs that can change depending on the amount of business the establishment does, such as the cost of food and drink
- **fixed costs** – costs that are always the same, such as rent, insurance and energy (they may increase or decrease at some point in time, however, depending on the business).

Variable costs: costs that change depending on the amount of business the establishment does, for example the amount of stock purchased.

Fixed costs: costs that are always the same, for example rent and energy.

Food forms a large percentage of the total costs in a catering establishment. It is therefore essential to know how much a recipe is going to cost to make and that dishes are costed accurately. Food costs need to be controlled so that the establishment makes a profit and stays in business.

When buying food, it is important to:

- order the correct amount of food
- order the best quality food at the best price
- monitor stock to make sure it is rotated, so that the oldest food is used up first.

Profit

REVISED

A business needs to be able to calculate how much profit it makes.

- **Gross profit** is the money that is left over when food costs have been deducted from sales income.
- **Net profit** is the money left over when all costs – material, labour and overheads – have been deducted from sales income.

> **Gross profit:** the amount of money made when the cost of goods (food and drink) sold has been deducted.
>
> **Net profit:** the amount of money made when all costs have been deducted.

> **Example**
>
> A restaurant business took £200,000 in food and drink sales over a year. Its total food costs were £55,000, labour costs were £53,500 and overheads were £39,100.
>
> Gross profit would be:
>
> £200,000 – £55,000 = £145,000
>
> Net profit would be:
>
> £200,000 – (£55,000 + £53,500 + £39,100) = £200,000 – £147,600 = £52,400

The economy

REVISED

The state of the economy can have an impact on a business in the following ways:

- **Value added tax (VAT)** – VAT is a consumption tax that has to be added on to a sale, raising money for the government from consumers' spending. The standard rate of VAT is currently 20 per cent. Some foods are exempt from VAT, but it has to be added to services. VAT is calculated quarterly and needs to be budgeted for, as it could be a large bill that will eat into profit. If the rate of VAT goes up, it will have an impact on businesses, which may need to charge more to cover this cost.

> **VAT:** a tax added to goods and services; the standard rate is currently 20 per cent.

- **Value of the pound and the exchange rate** – if the rate of exchange is good for consumers in other countries, they may choose to travel to the UK and spend money in the hospitality and catering sector. UK customers may stay in the UK if the exchange rate is poor.
- **Supply and demand** – if food production is affected by bad weather conditions, the cost of ingredients could increase due to the lack of food being available or a greater need for imported food.
- **Strength of the economy** – when the economy is strong, customers have more money to spend on leisure activities and eating out; when the economy is weak, customers may not have as much disposable income to spend.

Environmental factors

Being an environmentally friendly business, by promoting **sustainability** and using as few natural resources as possible, appeals to customers, and more customers should mean more profit. Keeping environmental costs to a minimum can also reduce overall costs, which also increases profit.

Hospitality and catering businesses can be inspected for sustainability by the Sustainable Restaurant Association (https://thesra.org). A good rating is one way that businesses can show customers that they care about sustainability.

> **Sustainable**: doing something in a way that maintains and improves the environment for future generations.
>
> **Seasonal foods**: foods that are only available at certain times of the year.

Seasonal foods

Buying foods when they are in **season** is more cost effective as they are in plentiful supply. Buying locally supports local farmers and also reduces the environmental cost of transporting foods over long distances. Customers like to know that restaurants are using local suppliers.

Sustainable methods of farming

Many farmers now work in a sustainable way; this means that they grow crops or rear animals in a way that maintains and improves the environment, for example by farming organically without the use of pesticides or fertilisers. Customers like to know where the food they are eating comes from and may choose to eat in a restaurant that uses sustainable suppliers.

Figure 1.14 Environmentally friendly businesses promote sustainability and use as few natural resources as possible

Reducing energy and water use

There are many ways that energy and water can be saved in the hospitality and catering industry; many of them also reduce costs and help to maximise profits. Methods include:

- installing solar panels
- installing double glazing and insulation to keep heating bills down
- using low-energy light bulbs
- buying energy-efficient appliances
- turning off lights when not in use or having automatic sensors for lights
- only using dishwashers and washing machines on a full load
- installing showers in hotel bedrooms rather than baths
- asking guests to reuse towels.

CERTIFICATION MARK

Figure 1.15 RSPCA assured logo

Food waste

Food waste can have a huge impact on profit. WRAP (the Waste and Resources Action Programme, www.wrap.org.uk) found that:

- 920,000 tonnes of food are wasted by the hospitality and food service sector every year
- 75 per cent of this waste – one in six meals – was avoidable
- on average, 45 per cent of food waste arises from preparation, 34 per cent from customer leftovers and 21 per cent from spoilage
- the average cost of avoidable food waste in a restaurant is £0.97 per meal.

Food that is left over can be reused to make another dish. This saves money as well as waste. Some ideas for using leftovers are:

- use leftover cake to make a trifle
- use leftover meat in a shepherd's pie
- use leftover chicken in a curry
- mash leftover potato and use it in fish cakes
- use leftover rice and pasta in salads
- fallen apples can be used to make pies, crumbles and preserves
- stale bread can be used to make breadcrumbs or a bread and butter pudding.

Controlling stock effectively can help to reduce food waste through spoilage – see page 34. The menu should be reviewed regularly to ensure that all stock ordered is used.

Accurate portion control to ensure there is little waste on customers' plates is also important. **Portion size** or control means controlling the quantity of food to be served to each customer. Controlling portion sizes will ensure that:

> **Portion size**: the amount of food recommended for one person to eat in one sitting.

- there is little wastage of food, which keeps costs down and helps the business to be profitable
- customers are happy – they feel they have value for money but the portion size is not so big that it cannot be finished.

If a customer leaves food on their plate they could be offered a 'doggy bag' to take home the uneaten food.

Packaging

Reducing packaging and the amount of plastic used saves energy, money and natural resources. Businesses can choose products with minimal packaging or packaging that can be recycled easily, as well as products made from biodegradable materials rather than plastic.

Technology

REVISED

Technology is rapidly evolving and changing, so it is important for businesses to keep up with it.

- Computers and computer systems are needed to run most businesses. All information can be stored and updated electronically. Orders can be taken electronically on tablets and sent directly to the kitchen.
- Booking of rooms, restaurants and meals can all be done online.
- Mobile phones can be used as door keys in hotels. This is done via an app on the phone and can be used instead of magnetic cards.
- Many establishments are going cashless accepting contactless or card payments only.
- Mailing/emailing lists can be used to send out promotional material and discounts.
- Social media is a powerful and often cost-effective way to promote a business.
- Recruiting staff online – for example, using Skype or Facetime for interviews reduces the need to travel to an interview, and takes up less time.

Figure 1.16 Taking an order with an electronic device

Emerging and innovative cooking techniques

- A number of different international cuisines are becoming increasingly popular in the UK, for example Sri Lankan and Burmese. Many customers like to try new foods and might want to visit these restaurants.

- Many people are cutting down on their meat intake and the popularity of vegan food is increasing. The Vegans Society estimated that there were about 600,000 vegans in the UK in 2018 – the number quadrupled between 2014 and 2018, with 42 per cent making the change in 2018. Many restaurants now offer meat-free and vegan dishes to cater for this rapidly growing market.

- Some bars are now serving green (healthy) juices and smoothies. This appeals to the growing market of health-conscious customers.

- Some restaurants are using vegetables instead of carbohydrate foods, either to reduce calories or to make dishes gluten free, for example:
  ○ spiralised courgettes instead of spaghetti
  ○ cauliflower that has been broken down using a food processor into a grain-like consistency to use instead of rice
  ○ cauliflower as a base for pizzas.

  Chefs are also looking for ways to reduce the fat, sugar and calorie content of their food. This appeals to those who want to go out for a meal but do not want to consume excess calories.

- The popularity of fermented foods – said to be rich in probiotics, which makes them good for gut health – is increasing. Good bacteria may improve digestion, boost immunity and promote a healthy weight. Examples include:
  ○ kimchi – a fermented vegetable dish from Korea
  ○ kefir – a fermented milk drink similar to yoghurt
  ○ kombucha – a fermented drink made from sweetened tea.

- The use of insects in cooking and insects used to make flour (for example cricket flour) is a growth area. Some customers may just want a different culinary experience, while others are interested in trying a more sustainable source of protein (less water and land are required to farm insects than livestock).

- Customers are attracted to fusions of different flavours and unusual tastes. The tea market is one example, with fusion flavours such as mushroom tea and cheese tea being developed. By expanding the selection of beverages, more customers might be attracted.

Customer demographics, lifestyles and expectations

Different customers have different needs when it comes to choosing somewhere to eat or stay.

Businesses need to take **demographics** into account. Demographics are information about the population of an area, such as the age, gender and income of the people. This information can help businesses to plan who their target market is going to be.

> **Demographics**: statistical information about the population, for example age, gender and income.

Customers have **expectations** when they choose somewhere to eat or stay. Different customers may have different expectations, as shown in Figure 1.17.

Figure 1.17 Customer expectations

Businesses also need to take into account the **lifestyle** of different groups of people. Lifestyle means how someone chooses to live and what they like to do.

> **Lifestyle**: how someone chooses to live and spend their money.

Table 1.8 shows the requirements of different groups of customers when they are choosing somewhere to eat.

Table 1.8 Requirements of different customers when choosing somewhere to eat

Customer group	Requirements
Disabled customers	Those with disabilities may need to be seated at a table on the ground floor rather than having to climb stairs. They may need help with carrying drinks or trays if the service is self-service or carvery style. Customers who use wheelchairs will need extra room to manoeuvre to and from their tables; this should be managed by waiting staff.

Table 1.8 Requirements of different customers when choosing somewhere to eat (continued)

Customer group	Requirements
Families with babies or young children	Babies and young children may need materials to keep them busy, for example colouring pencils and paper. They may also appreciate child-size cutlery, bibs and high chairs. They need a special menu with smaller portions.
Elderly customers	Older people may need extra time to order and help with ordering. They may also need smaller portion sizes.
Dietary needs or allergies	Customers with special dietary needs may need to check which allergens are included in which dishes on the menu if these are not clearly displayed.
Business customers	May need service to be quick.
Single customers	May want a table to themselves away from larger groups.

Table 1.9 shows the requirements of different groups of customers when they are choosing somewhere to stay.

Table 1.9 Requirements of different customers when choosing somewhere to stay

Customer group	Requirements
Disabled customers	Those with disabilities may need to be on the ground floor; they can be on higher floors with accessible lifts or ramps, however. They will need bathroom facilities with rails and a walk-in shower. It is useful if the accommodation has toilet facilities on the same floor as the restaurant.
Families with babies or young children	Will need a family room with sufficient beds or a cot
Elderly customers	May prefer to be on the ground floor or to have easy access to the lift. They may also prefer a walk-in shower to a bath.
Business customers	May need Wi-Fi or conference facilities.
Single customers	May want a double room with single occupancy to give them more space.

Customer service

- Each customer should receive excellent service every time they visit a restaurant or hotel.
- If customers are happy with the service, they are more likely to return.
- Well-run restaurants will provide ongoing training for staff to ensure they are providing the level of service customers expect. All staff should understand what excellent service is, and ensure all customers are well looked after and happy to return again.
- All customers should be treated as valued customers, with kindness and respect, regardless of their appearance or background.
- Staff should be smart and welcoming. You need to make sure the customer's first impression is a positive one.
- The body language and manner of staff should always be polite, respectful, friendly, sincere, patient and attentive. It is always good to smile and make eye contact.
- When orders are taken, it is important to read the order back to the customer to make sure you have heard the order correctly and it is accurate.
- Poor customer service will mean that customers don't return, which could cause the business to fail.

Competition

A business always needs to be aware of its competition. Competition is another business that provides a similar product or service to the same target customers.

A number of strategies could be used by a business to ensure that they attract and retain customers ahead of their competitors, including:

- monitoring the competition regularly – visiting the competitor as a customer, checking their website, reading comments on sites such as TripAdvisor
- offering competitive prices, deals and discounts
- evaluating your own business – ensure you are giving value for money and high-quality service
- having a clear advertising strategy and an up-to-date website – make sure images are clear and that the website is easy to navigate
- looking for a competitive advantage – this is a distinguishing feature you have that can give you an advantage over your competitors, for example a star chef; a fast, reliable home delivery service; an original menu; using high-quality organic products; or offering a wide selection of vegan choices.

Trends

A **trend** is a general direction in which something is developing or changing. It is crucial to keep an eye on current trends in hospitability and catering to help your business to evolve and develop.

> **Trend:** the general direction in which something is changing.

Some current trends in hospitability and catering are:

- Events management – for example wedding and conference planning – is a growing area within the sector.

- Independent restaurants and restaurants that offer customers something unique are likely to be the most successful, along with those that adopt new trends and introduce relevant technology.
- Larger pubs are doing well, particularly those with added letting rooms.
- Micro-pubs, tap rooms and pop-up bars are becoming popular.
- Rum is fast becoming a popular spirit, with increasing interest in British rums as well as traditional Caribbean rums.
- Large shopping centres are now hosting street food businesses.
- Communal dining halls and market halls are becoming popular, often located in old buildings. Altrincham Market House, for example, hosts themed markets with regional food producers; it has a canteen where people can eat from a variety of independent food operators.
- Eating where you shop (deli shops with bars and dining) and butcher–bistro places are becoming popular, for example The Butcher's Tap in Marlow owned by chef Tom Kerridge.
- Low- or no-alcohol drinks – mocktails, smoothies, juices.
- Many businesses are reducing the amount of packaging and plastic that they use, making changes such as replacing plastic cutlery with recyclable wooden ones, restricting serviettes, and using paper straws rather than plastic ones.

Figure 1.18 A food market

Political factors

REVISED

Policies, laws and regulations that govern how businesses operate all have an impact on the hospitality and catering industry.

Brexit

Currently there is much uncertainty about the UK leaving the EU – Brexit. This could have a number of impacts on the industry:

- If the cost of imported food rises, chefs may look to source more ingredients from the UK or outside the EU.
- EU nationals make up 40 per cent of the UK's hospitality and catering workforce; employers will need to review alternative staffing if the number of European workers declines.
- The value of the pound fluctuates according to the political situation.

Licensing laws

In England and Wales, the Licensing Act 2003 is the legislation used to license premises for the sale of alcohol. It requires a business to have a licence to serve alcohol, sets out its trading hours, and requires it to sell alcoholic beverages responsibly: checking ID and only selling to those over 18 years of age.

Employment laws

Employment rights are set out in a number of acts and regulations. Employees have the right to work in an environment free from discrimination and harassment. They also have the right to equal opportunities, fair wages and fair treatment, regardless of their race, religion, gender, sexual orientation and disability.

Health and safety regulations

These acts protect employees from harm. They are covered in more detail in Learning objective 3, Understand how hospitality and catering provision meets health and safety requirements, starting on page 47.

Media

The media has a variety of uses in the hospitality and catering industry. It can be used to promote and advertise businesses, and can used as a forum for customers' reviews.

Table 1.10 Uses of media

Media	Use
Internet search engines/maps	To look up places to eat in the local area. It is important for a business to have an online presence; if they are not on the internet, customers may not be aware of them and go elsewhere.
Websites	Websites are used to promote and advertise a business; many people use the internet when researching where to eat or stay.
Social media	Businesses receive feedback from customers on sites such as TripAdvisor. Photos of food can be shared on social media sites such as Instagram; if these are positive, it can influence whether customers visit or not.
Delivery	Sites such as Deliveroo and Just Eat can be used to find a restaurant, order food online and have it delivered; this will increase orders and, therefore, increase profits.

Exam tip

Create a mnemonic to help you remember the 12 factors affecting the success of hospitality and catering providers, for example:
- **Chefs** (costs)
- **Plan** (profit)
- **Educated** (economy)
- **Earlobes** (environmental)
- **Then** (technology)
- **Expect** (emerging and innovative cooking techniques)
- **Creative** (customer demographics and lifestyle)
- **Chocolate** (customer service)
- **Chillies** (competition)
- **To** (trends)
- **Peak** (political factors)
- **Media** (media)

Typical mistake

Learn the differences between each factor carefully, taking care as some overlap (for example technology and media, costing and competition, economy and politics). When asked to describe the effect the economy can have on the success of a business, students sometimes focus on politics instead; make sure you focus on the area the question asks for.

tripadvisor

Figure 1.19 Social media can be used to review businesses

Revision activity

Create a mind map of the 12 factors affecting the success of hospitality and catering providers outlined in this chapter. Elaborate on the 12 factors and draw images to help you remember them.

Now test yourself

1 Define the term 'fixed costs'. (2 marks)
2 Define the term 'net profit'. (2 marks)
3 State three ways in which a business can reduce its use of energy and water. (6 marks)
4 Describe three strategies that a hospitality and catering business could use to attract and retain customers. (6 marks)
5 State one change that a restaurant could make to reduce plastic use when serving food. (1 mark)

Answers and quick quizzes at **www.hoddereducation.co.uk/myrevisionnotes**

Unit 1 LO2 Understand how hospitality and catering provision operates

2.1 The operation of the kitchen

Layout

REVISED

The size and space of a kitchen should enable staff to work:

- safely
- efficiently
- in comfort.

The correct layout of a kitchen is crucial in maintaining high standards of food hygiene, and to ensure that there is enough space for everyone to work effectively and quickly to manage orders.

The main considerations are to:

- design an efficient workflow (see below)
- provide adequate work space so that staff do not get in each other's way
- create appropriate sections to avoid the risk of cross-contamination, for example vegetable preparation and washing-up areas should be separate from food preparation and service
- ensure access to all areas
- determine the number, size and type of equipment required.

Figure 2.1 A catering kitchen

Workflow

REVISED

The workflow should be in one direction – backtracking and crossover of materials and products must be avoided. The workflow shown in Figure 2.2 should be taken into consideration when designing a catering kitchen.

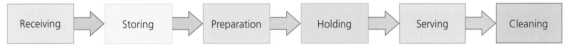

Figure 2.2 Workflow

It is important that the workflow is achieved by:

- minimum movement and backtracking
- effective use of space
- effective use of equipment
- minimum expenditure of time and effort.

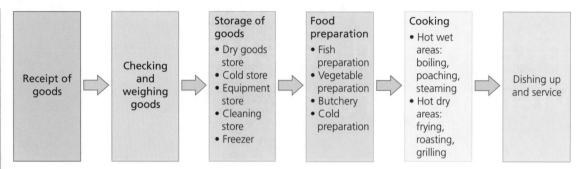

Figure 2.3 An efficient workflow pattern

Operational activities

The operational activities that occur in a catering kitchen follow the efficient workflow:

1 Goods are received and stored.

2 Food is prepared for cooking.

3 The food is cooked.

4 The food is dished up and presented for service.

5 Service – serving the food to the customers.

6 Cleaning and maintaining the kitchen area.

Equipment and materials

Large kitchen equipment – such as ovens, walk-in fridges and freezers, floor-standing mixers, deep fat fryers and sinks – are expensive, so initial selection is important. The following questions should be considered before each item is purchased or hired:

● Overall dimensions – will it fit in the kitchen?

● Weight – can the floor support the weight, does it need moving, is it too heavy to carry?

● Fuel supply – is the existing fuel supply sufficient to take the increase?

● Drainage – are there adequate facilities where necessary?

● Water – is it to hand where necessary?

● Use – does the food to be produced justify good use?

● Capacity – can it cook the required quantities of food?

● Time – can it cook food in the time available?

● Ease – is it easy for staff to handle, control and use properly?

● Maintenance – is it easy for staff to clean and maintain?

● Attachments – is it necessary to use additional equipment or attachments?

● Extraction – does it require extraction facilities for fumes or steam?

Figure 2.4 Large free-standing mixer

● Noise – does it have an acceptable noise level?

● Construction – is it well made, safe, hygienic and energy efficient? Are all handles, knobs and switches sturdy and heat resistant?

● Appearance – does it look good and fit in with the overall design? This is particularly important if it is to be on view to customers.

● Spare parts – are replacement parts easily obtainable?

Large equipment

Table 2.1 describes the use of large equipment in the kitchen.

Table 2.1 Large equipment used in a professional kitchen

Large equipment	Use
Convection (fan-assisted) oven	The fan circulates hot air, making it very efficient and cooking food consistently Used for baking and roasting
Microwave oven	Cooks food quickly Useful for reheating
Gas hob	These hobs have an exposed flame that is easy to regulate Used for cooking food in saucepans, frying pans and griddles
Induction hob	These energy-efficient hobs only heat up when in contact with a stainless-steel pan; they turn off and cool down quickly once the pan is removed Used for cooking food in saucepans, frying pans and griddles
Deep fat fryer	A thermostatically controlled container filled with oil and heated with an electric element Used to deep fry food
Salamander	A grill heated from above by gas or electricity Used to grill foods, for example steaks and bacon
Pressure steamers	Cook large quantities of food quickly by adjusting the pressure inside the steamer Used for cooking casseroles and vegetables
Under-heated grills	These grill food, such as steak or chicken, quickly from below Food can be moved on these grills to make a criss-cross pattern called a quadrillage
Refrigerator or chill room	To keep **high-risk food** such as meat, fish and dairy products chilled between 1 and 5°C
Freezer	Keeps food frozen at –18°C
Blast chiller	Used to cool or freeze hot food quickly

Figure 2.5 **Induction hob**

Figure 2.6 **Pressure steamer**

> **High-risk foods**: foods in which bacteria grow rapidly.

Small equipment

Table 2.2 describes the use of small equipment in the kitchen.

Table 2.2 Small equipment used in a professional kitchen

Small equipment	Use
Liquidiser or blender	Blends solid food into liquid, such as soups and smoothies
Hand-held food mixer	Used to beat and whisk smaller amounts of food quickly such as batters, cakes and biscuits
Table-top mixer	Used to beat and whisk larger quantities of food They often have attachments such as a dough hook to knead bread or a mincer for meat
Mincer	A stand-alone piece of equipment that minces meat into small pieces
Food processor	Used to mix, chop, slice and grate
Peelers	Used to take the skin off fruit and vegetables

Figure 2.7 Mincer

Utensils

A range of utensils are used in a catering kitchen, including:

- baking tins
- bowls
- colanders
- colour-coded chopping boards
- frying pans
- jugs
- knives
- ladles
- rolling pins
- saucepans
- sieves
- spatulas
- spoons
- woks.

Materials

Materials that are frequently used in a catering kitchen include:

- detergents – to remove dirt and grease
- disinfectant – to destroy bacteria
- first aid kit
- handwash and paper towels or hand driers
- kitchen cloths – disposable cloths are often used as they can be thrown away after use
- kitchen paper, foil, cling film, parchment paper, bin liners
- mops, dustpan and brushes, brooms, aprons
- oven gloves
- sanitiser – usually in the form of a spray for cleaning and disinfecting
- tea towels.

Stock control

REVISED

- All materials, ingredients and equipment used in a catering kitchen are called **stock**.
- Correct storage is important to ensure that ingredients to remain in the best condition, and are therefore safe to eat.

> **Stock:** all materials, ingredients and equipment used.

- All deliveries of food should be checked and moved to the most appropriate area within 15 minutes of delivery.
- The **first in, first out (FIFO)** policy should always be used to ensure that older stock is used up first. Dates on packaging need to be checked when deliveries are placed into stores.

FIFO: first in, first out policy – used to ensure that older stock is used up first.

Documentation and administration

REVISED

Table 2.3 outlines the necessary documentation and administration for a catering kitchen.

Table 2.3 Documentation and administration required in a catering kitchen

Documents	Description
Bin cards	Labels attached to stock items such as flour and sugar
	The bin card should show how much there is and how much has been used, so it can be reordered when running low
Stock ledger	A detailed list of all the stock, usually kept on a computer
Requisition stock book	Issued to each department to draw stock out from the store for the kitchen
Order book	For ordering stock
Delivery notes	For checking all the necessary details when food is delivered, such as the amount delivered and the price of each item
Invoices	For goods ordered
Food safety documentation	Temperature charts, for example for checking and recording fridge temperature
	Food hygiene and safety regulations
Health and safety documentation	Health and safety certificates for staff
	Accident book to record any accidents at work

Staff allocations

REVISED

The term **kitchen brigade** describes the organisational hierarchy of staff in a professional kitchen. Staff are allocated roles and responsibilities according to their qualifications and experience. Job roles are discussed on page 14.

Kitchen brigade: the organisational hierarchy of staff in a professional kitchen.

Executive chefs and head chefs are in charge of the kitchen brigade and make the decisions about where staff should be allocated and how many staff are required for each shift.

Dress code

REVISED

The term **dress code** describes a set of rules specifying the type of clothing to be worn by people under specific circumstances. Any chef should look clean and professional. The protective clothing worn must be clean, hygienic and in a good state of repair. This is important to prevent the transfer of bacteria from dirty clothing to food. The uniform should not be worn outside of the catering premises as bacteria from the outside can be carried in the kitchen.

Dress code: a set of rules outlining the clothing that needs to be worn by people.

Hat or hairnet

Long hair is tied back

Clean teeth

Clean-shaven

Chef's jacket, preferably with long sleeves

Blue plaster used to cover any cuts

Clean hands and nails

Apron from waist to knee

Baggy chef's trousers

Safety shoes with steel toe caps

Figure 2.8 A chef's clothing

A chef should wear:

- a jacket with long sleeves, usually double-breasted, made from cotton to stay cool while still protecting the chef from heat, burns and scalds
- trousers, which should be loose fitting for comfort and made from cotton to keep cool; loose fitting trousers can be removed easily if hot liquids are spilled on them
- apron – this is worn around the waist, over the trousers, as added protection
- hat – called a **toque**, which is worn to prevent hair from falling into food
- neckties – these used to be worn to prevent sweat from dripping into food; they are not worn as often now due to improved ventilation in kitchens
- safety shoes – should have steel toe caps in case a knife or hot food is dropped on the feet
- kitchen cloth – tucked in the apron, kept dry for handing hot pans and equipment.

> **Toque**: a chef's hat.

Safety and security

REVISED

Health, safety and security measures are put in place to prevent illness and accidents, and to ensure that workers are safe and secure. For more details, see Learning objective 3, Understand how hospitality and catering provision meets health and safety requirements, which starts on page 47.

Figure 2.9 Factors affecting health, safety and security in a catering kitchen

Now test yourself

TESTED ☐

1 Explain two points that need to be taken into consideration when designing the layout of a kitchen. (2 marks)
2 What is the correct workflow order? (6 marks)
3 What is a salamander? (2 marks)
4 Explain why FIFO is an essential part of stock control. (2 marks)
5 Explain why safety shoes should be part of a chef's uniform. (2 marks)

2.2 The operation of front of house

Layout

REVISED ☐

Front of house covers the following areas:

- reception (usually only present where there is overnight accommodation or conferences and events are taking place)
- bar
- lounge
- dining area
- toilets and cloakroom.

Restaurants and hotels can be busy, with customers moving around between different areas. There should be a logical layout so that people can move from one area to another easily. Reception should be clearly signposted, and ideally lead on to the bar, lounge, dining areas and toilets. Larger establishments may have a dedicated floor for reception and another for dining.

Figure 2.10 A busy restaurant

Workflow

Workflow in front of house describes the flow of food and drinks from the catering kitchen and bar to customers in the dining areas, bars or lounges.

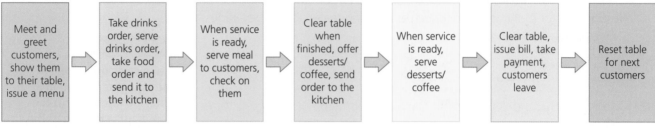

Meet and greet customers, show them to their table, issue a menu	Take drinks order, serve drinks order, take food order and send it to the kitchen	When service is ready, serve meal to customers, check on them	Clear table when finished, offer desserts/ coffee, send order to the kitchen	When service is ready, serve desserts/ coffee	Clear table, issue bill, take payment, customers leave	Reset table for next customers

Figure 2.11 An efficient workflow pattern for front of house

Operational activities

Operational activities that occur front of house include:

- reception – where customers check in and out, book tables and find out what facilities are offered both in the establishment and in the local area
- lounge – there is usually a social area where guests can relax with a drink or wait for their table
- bar – an area where drinks can be ordered; there are usually bar stools, tables and chairs
- restaurant/dining area – an area where guests can sit and eat a meal
- toilets and cloakroom – where guests can leave coats and use the facilities.

Figure 2.12 Checking in at reception

Equipment and materials

A range of equipment is needed in the different areas of front of house:

- reception – IT facilities for checking in and out, telephones, paper and pens, information about facilities in the establishment and in the local area
- lounge –furniture for the customers to use such as settees, chairs, tables, lamps and TVs
- bar – drinks measures, ice buckets, tongs, a range of glasses, coffee- and tea-making facilities, tills, menus, and a range of alcoholic and non-alcoholic drinks
- restaurant and dining area – table-top equipment such as salt and pepper grinders, flowers, candles, coasters and table mats, cutlery and crockery
- toilets and cloakroom – tissues, paper towels or driers, toilet roll, hand soap and hand cream.

Materials are also needed for housekeeping and cleaners working behind the scenes, for example:

- cleaning equipment for cleaning rooms and the restaurant
- mops, dustpans and brushes, brooms, vacuum cleaners
- bin liners
- handwash and paper towels or hand drier
- first aid kit.

Stock control

Stock for front-of-house use needs to be monitored in exactly the same way as stock for use in the kitchen, although it is likely that a different person will be in charge of monitoring it. Similarly, different people will probably be responsible for monitoring stock such as cleaning materials and beverages (wines, spirits and non-alcoholic drinks).

Documentation and administration

Table 2.4 shows the documentation and administration necessary for front of house.

Table 2.4 Documentation and administration required in front of house operations

Documents	Description
Stock ledger	A detailed list of all the stock, usually kept on a computer
Requisition stock book	Issued to each department to draw stock out from the store for front of house
Order book	For ordering stock
Delivery notes	For checking all the necessary details when materials are delivered
Invoices	For services and goods ordered
Services used	For example, laundry of sheets and towels
Financial and budget information	Overseeing the spending in all departments
Health and safety documentation	Health and safety certificates for staff Accident book to record any accidents at work
Employees	Documentation on all employees, including training records, sickness and accidents
Customer documentation	For checking customers in and out, feedback, and management of events and conferences

Staff allocations

Staff are allocated roles and responsibilities in front of house according to their qualifications and experience. Job roles are discussed on page 14.

The manager of a hotel has overall responsibility for staff in front of house, but it is likely that staff would be allocated roles and responsibilities by the head housekeeper, head receptionist or head waiter.

Dress code

REVISED

Front-of-house staff have to look smart and clean to present a positive image. They often have a corporate uniform.

Room attendants have a uniform covered by an apron for cleaning duties.

Waiting staff and bar staff have a specific dress code, designed to look smart and be hygienic and safe:

- usually a black skirt/trousers and white shirt/blouse
- long sleeves to cover arms in case of spillages and burns
- low-heeled black shoes for comfort
- long hair tied back
- apron on top of uniform to protect from hot food/drink and spillages
- cloth tucked in waistband to use if carrying hot plates and dishes.

Figure 2.13 Dress code for waiting staff

Safety and security

REVISED

Health, safety and security measures are put in place to prevent illness and accidents, and to ensure that workers are safe and secure. For more details see Learning objective 3, Understand how hospitality and catering provision meets health and safety requirements, starting on page 47.

Figure 2.14 Factors affecting health, safety and security in front of house

Revision activity

Copy and complete this revision table adding in the operational activities of both the catering kitchen and front of house.

	Catering kitchen	Front of house
Layout		
Workflow		
Operational activities		
Equipment and materials		
Stock control		
Documentation and administration		
Staff allocations		
Dress code		
Safety and security		

Using your table, make a note of the differences and similarities of each section.

Exam tip

Make sure you understand the differences and similarities between the catering kitchen and front of house.

Typical mistake

Be sure to read questions carefully. Make sure you know which aspect of operational activity the question is referring to: is it for the kitchen brigade or front of house?

Now test yourself

TESTED

1 Identify the five areas that the front of house covers. (5 marks)
2 State three pieces of equipment that are needed in a bar. (3 marks)
3 Describe one responsibility of a barista. (2 marks)
4 Identify two pieces of clothing a waiter or waitress would wear. (2 marks)
5 State one responsibility of a housekeeper. (2 marks)

2.3 How hospitality and catering provision meet customer requirements

Different customers

A hospitality and catering business cannot operate without customers, so meeting customer requirements is of the utmost importance. There are three main groups of customers: those who are there for leisure activities, those who are there for business or corporate customers, and local residents.

Leisure

Leisure customers are those who are visiting a residential establishment for:

- holiday – a break away from their home and the area where they live
- tourism – visiting a specific place
- sports activities – golf, gym, walking, water-based activities
- eating – they may wish to eat in the establishment but also want to explore eating places in the local area.

Figure 2.15 Leisure facilities at a hotel

Business/corporate

Corporate means a large business that is run by a group of people. A **business** is smaller and usually run by one person or a few people.

Business or corporate customers are those who are visiting a residential establishment for:

- meetings
- conferences
- exhibitions
- trade shows
- staff training.

> **Corporate:** relating to a large business (corporation).
>
> **Business:** a company that is smaller than a corporation.

Local residents

Local residents may visit the establishment to eat in the restaurant or to use other facilities. They are unlikely to stay overnight.

Customer needs

All customers have different needs and requirements. Hospitality and catering establishments should aim to ensure that these specific needs are met.

Table 2.5 The needs of different customer types

Type of customer	Possible customer needs
Leisure	Facilities such as a pool, gym or spa, sporting activities such as golf
	Local maps
	Tourist information
	Sightseeing information
Business or corporate	Pick up/taxi from the airport
	Express check in and out
	Business centre or lounge with IT facilities and Wi-Fi
	Trouser press and laundry service
	Financial newspapers and magazines
	High level of food and beverage facilities, personalised service
	Fine dining option
	Conference rooms
	Access to leisure facilities
Local resident	Access to facilities such as a pool, gym or spa, sporting activities such as golf
	Ability to book a table for lunch or dinner only

Customer satisfaction is crucial in running a successful business. Staff should be friendly and approachable; a smile and good manners are essential to make customers feel at ease and to make them feel welcome. Customers who are satisfied will want to return, so it is important to make them feel that:

- you have put their needs first
- they are valued and important
- they are safe and comfortable.

LO2 Understand how hospitality and catering provision operates

Customer expectations

Customers will have expectations that their needs are going to be met. These might include:

- **Value for money** – that the price they pay for a meal, service or a room will be fair. Note that this does not necessarily mean cheap – a room in a luxury hotel will be expensive but the extra facilities may mean that the price is still fair.

- **Reliability** – that the service they get will be as promised in the initial booking or order. If room service is advertised as taking 20 minutes, then it should arrive within 20 minutes.

- **Advice and help** – that they will be given any help and advice when needed. A receptionist should be able to explain where all the facilities are and how to get to their room. Waiting staff should be able to describe all of the items on a menu.

- **Accuracy** – that what they order is what they get. If they booked a room with a walk-in shower rather than a bath, then that is the room they would expect to be given.

- **Health, safety and security** – that the hospitality and catering establishment will have a duty of care towards its customers to ensure their safety, health and well-being.

- **Complaints or problems dealt with correctly** – sometimes things can go wrong and problems can occur; staff must be able to deal with them efficiently and to the satisfaction of the customer.

Figure 2.16 **Customer expectations**

Customer trends

Customers' requirements have changed over time and will continue to change and evolve. Current customer trends include:

- the use of technology and smartphones to book and order services
- the use of social media for information and communication
- ordering food online for delivery
- increased awareness of environmental issues – customers are interested in food provenance (where the food comes from) and in establishments' food waste policies
- increase in the numbers of vegetarians and vegans, and a subsequent increase in the number of restaurants catering for them
- menus offering healthier options, reliable allergy information and a variety of choices for people with food intolerances (for example to gluten and dairy).

Equality

Equality Act 2010

The **Equality** Act of 2010 protects customers from direct **discrimination** on the basis of:

- age
- disability
- gender reassignment
- pregnancy and maternity (which includes breastfeeding)
- race – this includes ethnic or national origins, colour and nationality
- religion or belief
- sex
- sexual orientation.

> **Equality:** being equal, especially in status, rights or opportunities.
>
> **Discrimination:** the unjust treatment of people, especially on the grounds of race, age or sex.

Businesses should treat everyone accessing their facilities or services fairly, regardless of their age, gender, race, sexual orientation, disability, gender reassignment, religion or belief, and must not make assumptions about their customers.

- A business cannot discriminate against mothers who are breastfeeding a child of any age.
- When providing facilities or services, it is unlawful to discriminate against or harass a transsexual person, whether or not they are under medical supervision.
- A business must not discriminate against a carer because they are caring for someone with a disability.
- Businesses need to make reasonable adjustments to help disabled individuals access their facilities and services. For example, where possible, adjustments should be made to stairways, steps, parking areas, entrances, exits, doors and gates, toilets and washing facilities, and lifts and escalators.
- Businesses must not allow their customers to be subjected to harassment which could disturb a person's dignity or create an intimidating or hostile environment for them.

L02 Understand how hospitality and catering provision operates

Customer rights

Consumer Protection Act 1987

This act gives you the right to claim compensation against the producer of a defective product if it has caused damage, death or personal injury. Manufacturers are legally obliged to put certain information on products, such as health and safety messages on equipment, that may be used by customers when eating out or staying in accommodation.

Consumer Rights Act 2015

This act states that all products must be:

- **Satisfactory quality** – goods shouldn't be faulty or damaged when you receive them.
- **Fit for purpose** – goods should be fit for the purpose they are supplied for.
- **As described** – the goods supplied must match any description given to you.

This legislation should ensure that a meal ordered matches the description given, or a room booked was fit for purpose, for example hot water is available in the bathroom.

General Data Protection Regulation 2016

When you buy goods and services, stay at a hotel or sometimes even just visit a website, the organisations you deal with may collect information and data about you, such as your name, address and date of birth.

Under the General Data Protection Regulation (GDPR) rules, businesses must now have a customer's consent to store this information and to use it for marketing purposes or to share it with other businesses.

> **Revision activity**
>
> Create mind maps of the needs and expectations of the different types of customers – leisure, business/corporate and local residents.

> **Typical mistake**
>
> Make sure you understand the differences between the needs of the three types of customers – leisure, business/corporate and local residents.

> **Exam tip**
>
> Practising past exam questions will help to improve your examination technique.

Now test yourself

TESTED

1. State two reasons why a business customer would visit a hotel. (2 marks)
2. Identify two needs of a local resident when visiting a large hotel. (2 marks)
3. List six expectations customers might have when visiting a catering or hospitality establishment. (6 marks)
4. State two grounds for discrimination that the Equality Act protects customers from. (2 marks)
5. Explain how the Consumer Rights Act protects customers. (2 marks)

Unit 1 LO3 Understand how hospitality and catering provision meets health and safety requirements

3.1 Personal safety responsibilities in the workplace

It is both the employer's and employee's responsibility to make sure they follow health and safety rules at work because:

- they help to prevent accidents
- they ensure the business is a safe place to work
- they ensure food is safe to eat.

Health and Safety at Work Act (HASAWA) 1974 REVISED

Employers must ensure that:

- equipment is tested for safety and correctly maintained
- chemicals are stored and used correctly by trained staff
- **risk assessments** are completed
- a **health and safety policy statement** is given to employees
- safety equipment and clothing are provided
- health and safety training is given and updated regularly.

Employees must ensure that they:

- work in a safe way so they don't put others in danger
- follow the health and safety rules set by their employer
- wear the safety clothing and equipment provided by their employer
- report anything that poses a health and safety risk, or something that could be a risk.

> **Risk assessment**: a way of identifying things that could cause harm to people in the workplace.
>
> **Health and safety policy statement**: a written statement by an employer of its commitment to health and safety for employees and the public.

Reporting of Injuries, Diseases and Dangerous Occurrences Regulations (RIDDOR) 2013 REVISED

These regulations require employers to report certain workplace incidents to the Health and Safety Executive (HSE) such as:

- death and serious injuries (for example serious burns)
- dangerous occurrences (for example near-miss events such as the collapse of equipment)
- work-related diseases (for example occupational dermatitis)
- flammable gas incidents (for example leaking gas)
- dangerous gas fittings (for example a faulty gas cooker).

Employers must also keep a record of any injury, disease or dangerous accident.

An employee must ensure that:

- they tell their line manager or union representative if they see any health and safety issue that concerns them
- any injuries at work are recorded in an accident book.

If nothing is done about a health and safety concern that an employee has reported, it can be reported to the HSE.

Control of Substances Hazardous to Health (COSHH) Regulations 2002

REVISED

The Control of Substances Hazardous to Health (COSHH) Regulations covers substances that are hazardous to health, for example:

- chemicals, for example cleaning materials
- fumes from machinery and cooking processes
- dusts, for example from icing sugar or flour
- vapours from cleaning chemicals, for example oven cleaner
- gases from cookers.

Any substances hazardous to health must be:

- stored, handled and disposed of according to COSHH Regulations
- identified on the packaging or container
- shown in writing and given a risk rating
- labelled as toxic, harmful, irritant, corrosive, explosive or oxidising.

An employer should ensure that employee use of and exposure to these substances is kept to a minimum.

An employee should ensure that they are trained in the use of these substances. They should take note of the international symbols that are used to identify the different types of substances and how they can cause harm.

Figure 3.1 **Symbols used to identify different types of substances and how they can harm people**

Manual Handling Operations Regulations (MHOR) 1992

REVISED

The Manual Handling Operations Regulations protect employees from injury or accident when they are lifting or moving heavy or awkward-shaped boxes. Items that are hot, frozen or sharp may also need to be carried in the hospitality industry – this is also covered by these regulations.

Employers must complete a risk assessment whenever items need to be moved, and provide adequate training.

Employees must be trained in correct manual handling techniques and lifting; moving equipment should be provided when appropriate.

Lifting

When handling boxes, cartons and trays, there is a correct way to lift:

- always keep your back straight when lifting
- bend your knees and use the strength in your arms
- never reach forward
- keep the item close to your body and make sure you hold the item firmly
- use protective clothing if there are sharp edges on boxes or cartons
- never attempt to carry items that are too heavy – always get help.

Answers and quick quizzes at www.hoddereducation.co.uk/myrevisionnotes

Figure 3.2 **The correct lifting technique**

Personal Protective Equipment at Work Regulations (PPER) 1992

REVISED

Personal protective equipment (PPE) is clothing or equipment designed to protect the wearer from injury. It is sometimes necessary when cleaning as the chemicals used in the workplace are often stronger than those you may use at home.

These regulations require employers to provide suitable high-quality protective clothing and equipment to employees who may be exposed to a risk to their health and safety while at work. This can include:

- **gloves** to protect hands from cleaning materials and metallic-style gloves to be used when cutting meat
- **goggles** to prevent eyes being splashed with chemicals
- **face masks** to prevent inhalation of any chemical or powder
- **long sleeves** to prevent contact with skin on arms
- **waterproof aprons** to be worn on top of clothing.

Signs to remind employees what PPE to wear and when should also be visible.

Employees are expected to attend training sessions on how to wear PPE and to wear it in the workplace as instructed by the employer.

> **Personal protective equipment (PPE):** clothing or equipment designed to protect people from harm.

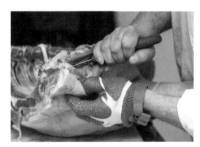

Figure 3.3 **Personal protective clothing may be needed when using sharp knives in butchery**

> **Typical mistake**
>
> If you have a question on health and safety responsibilities, check whether it is asking about the employer or the employee's responsibilities. It will make a difference to your answer.

> **Revision activity**
>
> Make sure you know the symbols for substances that can cause you harm. Make some revision cards with the hazard symbol on one side and what it means on the other.

Now test yourself

TESTED

1 State three reasons why everyone should follow health and safety rules at work. (3 marks)
2 List three rules for employers from the Health and Safety at Work Act 1974. (3 marks)
3 What does RIDDOR stand for? (1 mark)
4 What does COSHH stand for? (1 mark)
5 List three examples of personal protective equipment. (3 marks)

> **Exam tip**
>
> Make sure that you understand the key elements of each of the health and safety regulations/acts for protection in the workplace.

3.2 Risks to personal safety in hospitality and catering

It is important to follow correct procedures to ensure the workplace does not affect your health or security.

Risks to health

Figure 3.4 Risks to health and personal safety

Risks to security

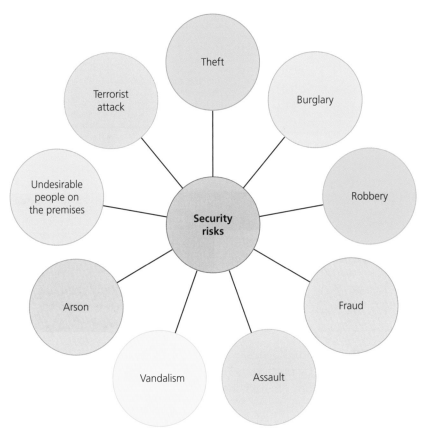

Figure 3.5 Risks to security

Levels of risk

A risk assessment should be carried out to identify **risks**. It is a way of identifying things that could cause harm to people in the workplace. All workplaces must have the necessary risk assessments in place. In a business there are five steps to risk assessment:

1 Identify the **hazard**.
2 Decide who might be harmed and how.
3 Evaluate the risks and decide on the **controls** (precautions).
4 Record the findings and implement them.
5 Review the assessment and update if necessary.

> **Risk**: how likely it is that someone could be harmed by a hazard.
>
> **Hazard**: something that can cause harm.
>
> **Control**: a way of reducing the risk of a hazard causing harm.

Calculating risk

It is possible to calculate whether the level of risk is high, medium or low. To do this, the hazard severity and the likelihood of it happening are given a score on a scale of one to five. They can then be multiplied together to give a level of risk. The overall aim is to remove or reduce the risk to an acceptable level (as close to 1 as possible).

LO3 Understand how hospitality and catering provision meets health and safety requirements

Table 3.1 Scales used to calculate the level of risk

Hazard severity	Likelihood of occurrence	Scale
Trivial	Remote (almost never)	1
Minor	Unlikely (occurs rarely)	2
Moderate	Possible (uncommon)	3
Serious	Likely (not frequent)	4
Fatal	Very likely (frequently)	5

Level of risk = hazard severity × likelihood of occurrence

Table 3.2 Levels of risk

Low risk 1–8	Medium risk 9–12	High risk 15–25
Continue but review regularly to ensure controls remain effective	Continue but implement additional controls where possible and monitor regularly	Stop the activity! Identify new controls Activity must not proceed until risks are reduced to a low or medium level

The risks identified in Figures 3.4 and 3.5 pose a threat to employees, suppliers and customers. These risks must be controlled by putting measures in place to ensure that they are all low or medium. No risks should be high.

Table 3.3 Potential risks to employees, suppliers and customers

Risks to employees	Risks to suppliers	Risks to customers
Stress, fatigue	Using equipment	Food poisoning
Using equipment	Trip hazards	Food allergies
Trip hazards	Food and drink spillages	Trip hazards
Food and drink spillages	Inadequate clothing worn	Food and drink spillages
Using hazardous chemicals	Moving and lifting objects	Fire and explosion
Inadequate clothing worn	Fire and explosion	Theft
Using electrical appliances	Injuries	Assault
Moving and lifting objects	Inadequate lighting	Undesirable people on the premises
Fire and explosion	Inadequate signage	
Bullying and harassment		
Injuries		
Inadequate lighting		
Inadequate ventilation		
Inadequate signage		
Theft		
Assault		
Undesirable people on the premises		

Now test yourself

TESTED ☐

1 What is a risk? (1 mark)
2 What is a hazard? (1 mark)
3 What is a risk assessment? (1 mark)
4 Identify six risks to the health and safety of an employee. (6 marks)
5 Identify two risks to the health and safety of a customer. (2 marks)

3.3 Personal safety control measures for hospitality and catering provision

Control measures for employees

REVISED ☐

The control measures outlined in Table 3.4 can be put in place to help protect employees' personal safety.

Table 3.4 **Control measures for employees**

Hazard	Control
Stress, fatigue	Employees need to be monitored closely and adequate rest breaks should be allocated
Using equipment	The instruction manual needs to be followed, with training given if needed
Trip hazards	Floors need to be clutter free; exits and entrances need to be clear
Food and drink spillages	Clear up spillages immediately and use warning signs
Using hazardous chemicals	Wear protective clothing where necessary; training should be given on the use of chemicals; chemicals should be stored correctly; COSHH regulations need to be followed
Inadequate clothing worn	The correct PPE should be worn at all times; wear aprons that are done up correctly; shoe laces should be tied up

Figure 3.6 **Green signs are used to guide people to fire escapes and emergency exits**

Table 3.4 Control measures for employees (continued)

Hazard	Control
Using electrical appliances	The equipment should be maintained and cleaned regularly; training should be given if necessary; it should be **PAT tested** regularly by a qualified electrician
Moving and lifting objects	Wear the correct PPE; training on safe lifting techniques should be given
Fire and explosion	Under the Fire Safety Order 2005, employers must ensure there is a low risk of fire and explosion by: ● having fire alarms and making sure they are tested regularly ● making sure escape routes are clear and adequately signed ● having suitable equipment such as fire extinguishers available
Bullying and harassment	Protocols and policies should be in place to ensure that this does not happen; there should be an open culture if anyone needs to report it
Injuries	Kitchens and restaurants can be dangerous places – there should be a first aid kit and a trained first aider
Inadequate lighting	Lighting must be bright enough to work safely in; if a light is broken it should be fixed
Inadequate ventilation	Good ventilation is needed in a catering kitchen; this is normally provided by extractor fans, which remove steam, heat and smells; the kitchen may be hot so drinking water should be available
Inadequate signage	Signs need to be clear and visible; staff need to be made aware of what the signs mean
Theft	A secure area should be available for staff to leave personal belongings
Assault	Train staff on how to deal with aggressive customers and diffuse volatile situations
Undesirable people on the premises	Have a security system to monitor who is entering the premises; any suspicious person should be reported; effective signing in and out procedures are required

PAT tested: all portable electrical appliances, including flexes and cables, need to be tested for safety by a qualified electrician.

Bullying and harassment: when someone constantly finds fault with someone else and criticises them, often publicly; bullying tends to consist of small incidents over a long period of time, whereas harassment is often one or two serious incidents.

Figure 3.7 All catering establishments should have a first aid kit

Table 3.5 Control measures for customers

Hazard	Control
Food poisoning	Hazard Analysis and Critical Control Point (HACCP) system put in place to ensure food prepared, cooked and served is safe to eat (see Section 4.3, Food safety legislation, page 63)
Food allergies	Detailed information must be given to customers on any allergens in the dishes
Trip hazards	Make sure areas where customers go are well lit and that there are no trailing wires or clutter on the floor
Food and drink spillages	Spillages must be cleared up straight away and the appropriate signage used
Fire and explosion	Emergency exits must be well lit and signposted; fire extinguishers should be in place and staff should be trained in how to use them
Assault	Staff should ensure the safety of customers if another person is aggressive
Theft/fraud	Ensure that card transactions are done in front of the customer; provide a secure place for their belongings
Undesirable people on the premises	Any suspicious person should be challenged and not allowed to mix with the customers

Revision activity

Make a series of revision cards with a hazard on one side and the control on the other side.

Exam tip

Remember the difference between a hazard and a control. A hazard is something that can cause harm; a control is a way of reducing the risk of a hazard causing harm.

Typical mistake

Check the question carefully – is it asking about employees, employers, suppliers or customers? Make sure your answer applies to the group being asked about.

Now test yourself

TESTED ☐

1 List six hazards that could occur in a catering kitchen. (6 marks)
2 What control would you put in place for moving and lifting objects? (2 marks)
3 What control would you put in place for using hazardous chemicals? (3 marks)
4 List four hazards that could affect customers. (4 marks)
5 What control would you put in place for theft and fraud from a customer? (2 marks)

Unit 1 LO4 Know how food can cause ill health

4.1 Food-related causes of ill health

Microbes

REVISED

Microbes are tiny micro-organisms that can contaminate food and spoil it, causing ill health. The micro-organisms discussed here are bacteria, yeasts and moulds.

Bacteria

- Bacteria are single-celled micro-organisms. Bacteria can be found everywhere around you: on your skin, in food, in soil, in water and in the air.
- Most bacteria are harmless, but some are **pathogenic** and can cause food poisoning. General food poisoning **symptoms** are vomiting (being sick) and diarrhoea.
- Other types of bacteria cause food to decay; these are called food spoilage bacteria, which cause food to smell and lose its texture and flavour.
- Bacteria grow best with warmth (around body temperature, 37 °C); they prefer moist conditions on neutral foods containing protein.

> **Microbes**: tiny micro-organisms, such as bacteria, yeasts and moulds, that can spoil food.

Figure 4.1 Pathogenic bacteria under a microscope (listeria)

> **Pathogenic**: harmful; pathogenic bacteria can cause food poisoning.
>
> **Symptom**: a sign or indication of an illness or disease.

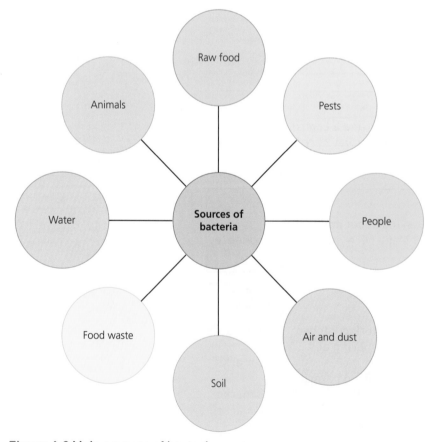

Raw food

Animals

Pests

Water

Sources of bacteria

People

Food waste

Soil

Air and dust

Figure 4.2 Main sources of bacteria

Yeasts

- Yeasts are single-celled fungi that reproduce by 'budding' – the yeast cell grows a bud, which becomes bigger until it eventually breaks off and becomes a new yeast cell.
- Yeast can grow in acidic, sweet foods; for example orange juice can ferment if it is not stored correctly, and honey can ferment if it is not pasteurised.
- Yeasts can grow with (aerobic) or without (anaerobic) oxygen.
- Yeasts prefer moist, acidic foods.
- Yeasts can grow in high concentrations of sugar and salt.
- Yeasts grow best in warm conditions (around 25–29 °C) but can also grow at fridge temperatures (0–5 °C).
- Yeasts are destroyed at temperatures above 100 °C.

Moulds

- Moulds are tiny fungi; they produce thread-like filaments that help the mould to spread around the food.
- Moulds grow in warm and moist conditions.
- Moulds grow easily on bread, cheese and soft fruits, and can grow on foods with high sugar and salt concentrations.
- Moulds grow best between 20 °C and 30 °C, but can also grow in the fridge (0–5 °C).
- Mould growth may be speeded up by high humidity and fluctuating temperatures.
- Moulds can grow on fairly dry food, such as hard cheese (for example Cheddar cheese).
- Moulds often spoil food such as bread and other bakery products.

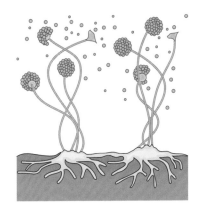

Figure 4.3 Mould growing

Chemicals
REVISED

Foods may be contaminated by chemical substances such as:

- cleaning fluids
- insecticides
- bleach.

These chemicals are extremely poisonous if swallowed.

Metals
REVISED

Aluminium

- Aluminium is one of the most common metals used in cookware as it is lightweight and conducts heat well.
- When aluminium surfaces are in contact with acidic foods, such as tomatoes and citrus fruits, the aluminium reacts and can leach (dissolve) into the food. This can give the food an unwanted metallic taste.
- While aluminium has been associated with Alzheimer's disease, there is no evidence that it causes the disease. The World Health Organization estimates that adults can consume more than 50 mg of aluminium daily without harm, so day-to-day exposure to aluminium from cooking is considered to be safe.

- Aluminium cookware can be anodised (hardened through a process that makes it unreactive) or coated with a less-reactive material, such as stainless steel, so that it does not react with food.

Copper

- Copper may be used in cups, pots and pans. It warms quickly and is the best conductor of heat.
- Copper and copper-alloy surfaces react with acidic foods, such as tomatoes and citrus fruits, and can leach (dissolve) into the food. High doses of copper can be toxic, so most copper pans are lined with stainless steel to avoid this happening.

Poisonous plants

REVISED

- Some mushrooms are poisonous, so you should pick mushrooms to eat unless you are 100 per cent sure of what they are. The death cap and autumn skullcap are two of the most poisonous. Consuming poisonous mushrooms can lead to pain in the area of the kidneys, thirst, vomiting, headache and fatigue.
- Many berries that grow wild are poisonous and should not be eaten. Yew berries, deadly nightshade and unripe elderberries are all poisonous. Consuming poisonous berries can lead to nausea, vomiting, stomach ache and diarrhoea, but it can also be fatal.
- Rhubarb leaves contain oxalic acid, which shuts down the kidneys and can be fatal; the stalks are safe to eat however.
- Glycoalkaloids are found in the leaves, stems and sprouts of potatoes. They can build up in potatoes if they left too long in the light, causing them to turn green. Eating glycoalkaloids can lead to cramps, diarrhoea and coma, and can prove fatal.
- If nuts and cereals get damp when they are stored, they can develop a mould that produces a **toxin** that can damage the liver.
- Dried kidney beans contain a toxin called lectin that makes them unsuitable for eating. Eating raw or inadequately cooked beans can lead to symptoms that indicate food poisoning. Kidney beans should be soaked and boiled for at least ten minutes to destroy the toxin.

> **Toxin**: a poison, especially one produced by micro-organisms such as bacteria, yeasts and moulds.

Allergies

REVISED

- A person with a food allergy experiences an allergic reaction when they eat or come into contact with specific foods.
- Allergic reactions are caused by the body's immune system reacting to the food and can be fatal. The symptoms of an allergic reaction are discussed in Section 4.5, Symptoms of food-induced ill health, on page 72.
- The most common foods that people may be allergic to are shown in Figure 4.4, but many other foods can cause an allergic reaction.

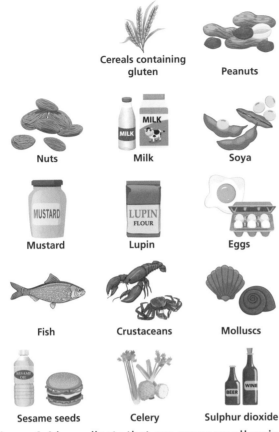

Cereals containing gluten

Peanuts

Nuts

Milk

Soya

Mustard

Lupin

Eggs

Fish

Crustaceans

Molluscs

Sesame seeds

Celery

Sulphur dioxide

Figure 4.4 Ingredients that can cause an allergic reaction

Intolerances

Some people have a sensitivity to certain foods. This is called a **food intolerance**. Eating these foods can cause symptoms such as nausea, abdominal pain, joint aches and pains, tiredness and weakness.

Lactose intolerance

- A person with a **lactose** intolerance cannot digest the sugar in milk called lactose.
- People with a lactose intolerance need to avoid all dairy products and foods that contain dairy products in their ingredients.

> **Food intolerance**: a sensitivity to certain foods; can cause symptoms such as nausea, abdominal pain, joint aches and pains, tiredness and weakness.
>
> **Lactose**: a sugar naturally found in milk.

Figure 4.5 Lactose-free products

> **Revision activity**
>
> Make a list of all the food-related causes of ill health.

Gluten intolerance

- Gluten is a protein present in a number of cereals including wheat, rye and barley.
- Wheat is an important and nutritious staple in the UK diet and is found in a number of foods including flour, baked products, bread, cakes, pasta and breakfast cereals.
- People with a gluten intolerance need to follow a gluten free diet.
- It is important not to confuse gluten intolerance with **coeliac disease**, which is an autoimmune disease caused by a reaction of the immune system to gluten. A person with coeliac disease is called a **coeliac**. For more information, see page 74.

Coeliac disease: an autoimmune disease caused by a reaction of the immune system to gluten.

Coeliac: a person who has coeliac disease.

Now test yourself   TESTED ☐

1. Name three microbes.   (3 marks)
2. Describe signs of food spoilage by mould and how it could be prevented.   (2 marks)
3. Describe how kidney beans should be cooked to avoid becoming ill.   (2 marks)
4. Describe the differences between a food intolerance and a food allergy.   (2 marks)
5. Name three foods that should be avoided by customers with a lactose intolerance. (3 marks)

4.2 The role and responsibilities of the Environmental Health Officer

Environmental Health Officers (EHOs) are responsible for carrying out measures to protect public health and to provide support to minimise health and safety hazards.

Environmental Health Officer (EHO): responsible for inspecting all premises involved in food production to ensure that health and safety hazards are minimised.

Role of EHOs   REVISED ☐

- They look after the safety and hygiene of food through all the stages of manufacture or production from distribution to storage and service.
- They help develop, co-ordinate and enforce food safety policies.
- They have the right to enter and inspect food premises at all reasonable hours and can visit without advance notice.
- They carry out routine inspections of all food premises in their area; the frequency of routine inspections depends on the potential risk posed by the type of business and its previous record – some high-risk premises may be inspected at least every six months, others much less often.
- They visit premises as a result of a complaint.
- They have powers of enforcement and can close businesses in extreme cases.

Figure 4.6 An environmental health officer checking premises

Answers and quick quizzes at **www.hoddereducation.co.uk/myrevisionnotes**

- They check that food producers handle all food hygienically so as not to give customers food poisoning.
- They check that food is being kept at the specific temperatures at which it should be stored or held.
- They check that staff are properly dressed, with clean nails, no jewellery, hair covered or tied back, and showing good hygiene habits.
- They review processes in the workplace, such as the handling of food, use of equipment, use of colour-coded boards, washing-up and disposal of waste.
- They inspect food stores – fridges, freezers and dry stores.
- They check stock rotation and temperature logs.
- They check that equipment is clean, well maintained and with safety notices if appropriate.
- They check the temperature of food when it is cooked with probes to ensure that it is at the correct temperature.
- They ask questions to check compliance with the law or good practice.
- They identify potential hazards.
- They review food safety management systems and plans.
- At the end of an inspection they give verbal feedback, discuss any problems and advise on possible solutions. They complete a report of inspection findings, which tells the business what **enforcement action** is to be taken.

> **Enforcement action**: action required by law following an inspection from an EHO.

Enforcement action

Enforcement action can range from verbal advice, informal or formal letters, and notices through to prosecution.

Formal Inspection letters

A Formal Inspection letter tells the food business which issues must be addressed to comply with the law. The EHO may revisit the business to check that the issues have been resolved.

Figure 4.7 **A hygienic food store**

Hygiene Improvement Notices

An EHO can serve a **Hygiene Improvement Notice** when they believe that a food business is failing to comply with food hygiene regulations. This notice will specify what is going wrong and what needs to be done by which date. The EHO will visit again to see if the required work has been done. If it has not improved, it can lead to a fine or imprisonment.

> **Hygiene Improvement Notice**: a notice that tells a business how to improve their food hygiene standards.
>
> **Hygiene Emergency Prohibition Notice**: notice served if there is a serious risk of harm; it stops unsafe practices immediately.

Hygiene Emergency Prohibition Notices

If an EHO believes that there is a significant risk to health or injury, a **Hygiene Emergency Prohibition Notice** may be served. The notice stops the use of unsafe equipment, processes or premises immediately. It can only be removed by an EHO once the issues have been addressed.

Voluntary closure

A food business may elect to close voluntarily to carry out improvements. However, should the business reopen before the improvements are completed, the EHO will serve a Hygiene Emergency Prohibition Notice.

Seizure and detention of food

EHOs have the power to inspect and seize food suspected of not meeting food safety regulations. Food is taken if there is suspicion that it is contaminated and is likely to cause food poisoning or disease. Seized food may undergo microbiological examination and testing.

Condemnation of food

In order to condemn or seize food, the EHO must present their findings to a court. They will consider the information and decide whether the food poses a risk to human health and whether or not to condemn it.

Voluntary surrender of food

The owner of a business may surrender unfit food to the EHO voluntarily. This would avoid the involvement of the court.

Revision activity

Read the following extract from a routine visit by an EHO to a fish and chip shop.

The owner was preparing the batter. He had a skin complaint and his neck and hands were covered in spots and blisters. He escorted the EHO into the food preparation area. The EHO put on a clean white coat and hat. She washed her hands in a small hand basin; soap, paper towels and cold water were available. It was a hot day and the back door was open. Two long ribbons of fly paper hung from the ceiling. An employee wearing a thin plastic apron was dealing with a delivery of fresh fish and frozen food.

Six large sacks of potatoes lay on the floor and were stacked against the wall. A mop bucket was filled with dirty water. Cleaning products were stored by the potatoes.

The premises had two large stainless-steel sinks. Each was filled with used equipment and utensils.

The EHO entered a large walk-in refrigerator. A long strip of cardboard had been placed on the floor. Her temperature probe revealed this was operating at the correct temperature of 5 °C. Fresh fish was stored on a top shelf uncovered and next to a tray of cooked pies.

Next the EHO inspected the hot holding area. The temperature dial on the hot holding cabinet indicated that it was at 75 °C; the EHO's own probe revealed a temperature of 65 °C. The cabinet contained a selection of pies, cooked fish and sausages.

1 Identify as many food safety and hygiene issues as you can.
2 Write a letter to the manager of the fish bar informing him of your concerns. Give instructions on how to improve food safety and hygiene.

Exam tip

Make sure you know the different stages of enforcement notices.

Now test yourself

TESTED ☐

1 How often can a premises classed as high-risk be visited? (1 mark)
2 Name four different types of enforcement action. (4 marks)
3 What is a Hygiene Improvement Notice? (1 mark)
4 What is a Hygiene Emergency Prohibition Notice? (1 mark)
5 Why might the owner of a food premises voluntarily surrender unfit food? (1 mark)

Typical mistake

Check the question – is it asking about the *role* or the *responsibility* of an EHO?

Answers and quick quizzes at **www.hoddereducation.co.uk/myrevisionnotes**

4.3 Food safety legislation

Food Safety Act 1990

- This act is concerned with all aspects of food production and sale.
- It affects everyone involved in the production, processing, storage, distribution and sale of food.
- It ensures that all food produced is safe to eat.
- The act states that it is an offence to make food sold for human consumption unsafe to eat.
- A food producer or retailer may not add any substance to food, or subject food to any process or treatment, which will make it harmful to health.
- An EHO may inspect any food intended for human consumption at all reasonable times. If the food is regarded as unfit for human consumption, it may be seized.
- The legislation also provides a defence for food producers, processors and retailers. They must prove that all reasonable precautions were taken to prevent a food safety incidence. This is called **due diligence**.
- Failure to take reasonable precautions can result in prosecution.
- Magistrates' courts may impose a fine, prison sentence or both for offences committed.

> **Due diligence**: reasonable precautions that should be taken to ensure that a business complies with the law.

Food Safety (General Food Hygiene) Regulations 1995

These regulations apply to food businesses and cover all activities involving food. The legislation clearly sets out the responsibility of food businesses to:

- produce food safely and make sure it is consistently safe to eat; food is unsafe if it is harmful to health and unfit for human consumption
- keep records of suppliers so that food can be traced; businesses must withdraw food that does not meet food safety requirements.

The whole food chain, from **farm to fork**, is covered by legislation. Farm to fork means that food can be traced through all the stages of production, processing and distribution back to the original source.

> **Farm to fork**: a system that allows food to be traced back to its original source.

The regulations require that food is stored, handled, cooked and served safely; that premises are clean and hygienic; and that people handling food follow basic hygiene rules.

Basic hygiene rules

- Don't cough or sneeze near food.
- Don't touch your head, especially your mouth, nose and ears.
- Wear the protective clothing and footwear provided by your employer.
- Don't brush your hair when wearing protective clothing or in any food areas.
- Long hair should be tied back and covered.
- Cuts and scratches should be covered with coloured waterproof plasters.
- Don't prepare food if you are unwell with a stomach bug or cough and cold, as you could spread bacteria onto food.

Record keeping

Detailed records need to be kept of:

- food safety management procedures
- training records of staff and staff illness reporting procedures
- cleaning schedules
- **pest control** and waste disposal contracts
- records of checks, problems found and action taken, for example a food temperature logbook
- list of suppliers.

Hazard analysis and critical control point

Hazard analysis and critical control point (HACCP) is a process that is designed to help you look at how you handle food and to put procedures in place to ensure that the food you produce is safe to eat.

Every business that produces, sells or serves food is required to have a HACCP plan in place with a written **food safety plan**. It is the responsibility of the owner of the business to develop an appropriate food safety management system based on HACCP.

HACCP systems should apply the following principles:

1 Create a flow chart or table showing each step in the preparation, making, serving and storing of each dish.

2 Each step should be analysed to identify the hazards. Hazards can be:

- ○ **physical** – foreign materials can cause injury to the consumer; these might be metal or plastic, or natural hazards such as bones in fish

- ○ **biological** – food can become infected by bacteria, which might lead to food poisoning

- ○ **chemical** – potentially dangerous chemicals such as cleaning fluids can contaminate food.

3 Identify what can be done to control (prevent) the hazard.

4 Set guidelines on how to ensure food is going to be safe to eat – these are known as **critical limits** – and keep a record of this.

5 When new dishes are made, there needs to be a HACCP review to ensure that they are safe to eat.

6 All the documentation relating to the HACCP needs to be kept safe.

Food safety plan

The following information should be included in a written food safety plan:

- purchase and delivery
- stock control
- storage and preparation
- chilled food
- frozen food
- cooking
- hot holding
- cooling
- reheating
- personal hygiene
- equipment and premises
- cleaning and maintenance
- pest control.

Hot holding is the process of keeping cooked food hot (above 63 °C). If the temperature falls below 63 °C there is a risk that harmful bacteria will multiply and cause food poisoning.

> **Pest control**: the regulation or management of a species defined as a pest, for example flies.
>
> **Hazard analysis and critical control point (HACCP)**: a food safety process in which every step in the manufacture, storage and distribution of a food product is analysed to ensure that the food is safe to eat.
>
> **Food safety plan**: practical steps to identify and control hazards in order to establish and maintain food safety.

Figure 4.8 A temperature probe

> **Hot holding**: keeping cooked food hot so that it is ready to be served.

Table 4.1 Food safety plan for hot holding

Hazard	Harmful bacteria can multiply if the temperature falls below 63°C
Safe hot holding plan	Cabinet and utensils are clean before use
	Preheat cabinet before use
	Keep hot food above 63°C
	Keep food hot only once
	Food must be piping hot throughout before hot holding begins (to 75°C)
	Food remains in cabinet and door is closed after use
Checking hot holding	Probe the temperature of the food daily – the core should be over 63°C
	Check that the temperature of the appliance is accurate daily
	Log temperatures in a temperatures book

Corrective action if there is a problem	For example, if the hot holding cabinet does not maintain safe temperatures for food products:
	● inform the manager there is a problem
	● increase the temperature of the cabinet or remove some food
	● if food has been in the **danger zone** for an unknown time it should be **destroyed**
	● if food has been in the danger zone for less than two hours, either:
	  – cool quickly and refrigerate food below 8°C, ideally between 2°C and 5°C
	  – reheat food quickly to 75°C and return to a correctly functioning appliance, maintaining temperature above 63°C
	● ring engineer on the number in the folder; request urgent call-out
	● replace equipment if necessary; supplier contact details are in the folder

Who is responsible for these checks?	Name of employee and their training needs

> **Danger zone**: temperatures between 5°C and 63°C, which allow the rapid growth of bacteria.

The plan in Table 4.1 suggests ways of managing this process and the checks to ensure that the hazards are controlled. As required by the legislation, there is a method of recording the checks.

Using this system can demonstrate the defence of 'due diligence' legally. To prove due diligence a business must be able to demonstrate that it took every possible reasonable step to achieve safe food. This may protect the owner of the business from prosecution.

It is likely that the court would demand written records to support the defence. These might include documents from the food safety plans. Other relevant documentation may include staff training records, temperature logs, cleaning schedules, supplier specifications, traceability systems, remedial action where food safety problems have arisen, and pest control measures.

Food labelling regulations

Food labels are used by businesses to provide information about their products. They are needed to:

- enable consumers to make informed decisions and choices, and to educate them about the food they choose to buy

- help us to store, prepare and cook the food we buy correctly

- identify the ingredients used in the food – if a consumer has a severe allergy to certain ingredients (for example nuts), they need to check if the food contains those ingredients

- establish the nutrient content of the food – if a consumer has a health condition such as diabetes or high blood pressure, they may want to check the sugar, fat, carbohydrate or salt content of the food

- identify the manufacturer's name and address, in case a customer wants to complain about the product, for example

- identify where the food comes from – some consumers may prefer to buy local produce.

Mandatory information required on labels

Mandatory information required on labels for prepacked foods is shown in Figure 4.9.

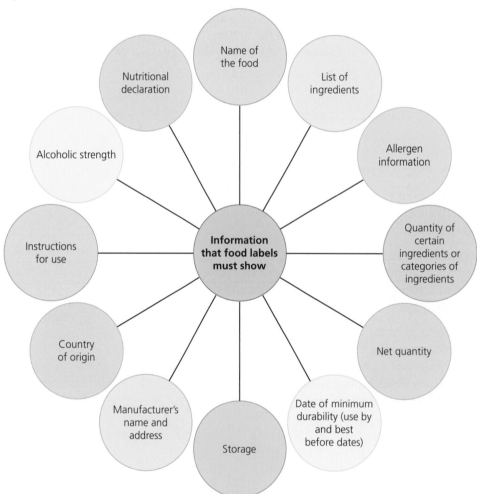

Figure 4.9 Information required on food labels

Non-prepacked food made by food catering businesses does not have to be labelled in the same way. They must provide clear allergen and intolerance information, but they do not have to provide a full list of ingredients.

Dates of minimum durability

Different types of dates are used to tell customers when the food should be consumed by:

- **Use-by date** – usually on high-risk foods such as soft cheeses, chilled meats, salads and sandwiches, which can go off quickly; it states the date that the food should be used by.
- **Sell-by or display-until date** – this date is aimed at shopkeepers rather than consumers; it is usually a few days before the use-by date to allow the consumer time to eat the food.
- **Best-before date** – these are given on foods that keep for longer, for example biscuits; the food should be eaten before this date for quality purposes, but it is not usually harmful to eat it after this date.

Nutritional labelling

Nutritional information must be expressed per 100 g or per 100 ml, and it must be listed in the following specific order:

- energy – stated in kilojoules (kJ) and kilocalories (kcal) per 100 g or 100 ml
- fat
- saturates
- carbohydrate
- sugars
- fibre (not required by law)
- protein
- salt
- vitamins and minerals – these must also be expressed as a percentage of the **reference intake (RI)**.

> **Reference intake (RI):** the maximum amount of calories/nutrients you should eat in a day.

Traffic light labelling

Traffic light labelling is a voluntary system that uses traffic light colours to indicate how healthy a product is at a glance in terms of fat, saturated fat, sugar and salt.

- **Red** – the food is high in something that consumers should try to cut down on in their diet; such foods should be chosen less frequently and eaten in small amounts.
- **Amber** – the food isn't high or low in the nutrient, so this is an acceptable choice most of the time.
- **Green** – the food is low in that nutrient; the more green, the healthier the choice.

Consumers should choose foods with more greens and ambers and fewer reds to ensure healthier choices.

Traffic light labels also give the amount of fat, saturated fat, sugars and salt in grams, the manufacturer or retailer's suggested 'serving' size, and information on the nutrient as a percentage of RI.

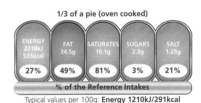

Figure 4.10 The traffic light label

Nutrition claims

There are strict rules about claims that can be made about food on its packaging so that consumers are not misled. For example, if the packaging says that the product is 'fat free', the product must not contain more than 0.5 g of fat per 100 g or 100 ml.

Any health claim that a manufacturer makes has to be reviewed to ensure it is accurate before it appears on the label.

Revision activity

Copy and complete the following table.

Information on a label	Reason why it is there
Name of the food	
Ingredients list	
Information on certain foods causing allergies or intolerances that were used in the manufacture or preparation of a food	
Net quantity of the food, weight or volume	
Date of minimum durability	
Any special storage conditions	
Name or business name and address of the food manufacturer	
Country of origin or place of provenance of the food (if required)	
Instructions for use	
Alcoholic strength by volume (if required)	
A nutrition declaration	

Exam tip

Look at labels on a variety of foods – cans, packets, frozen and chilled. This will help you remember what is on a label and remind you of why it is there.

Typical mistake

Read the details of the question carefully. If the question is asking you about cooking and serving, then focus on those aspects only.

Now test yourself

TESTED

1 Why is 'farm to fork' important? (2 marks)
2 Explain what HACCP is. (2 marks)
3 Identify the three types of hazards. (3 marks)
4 State three reasons why food labels are important to a consumer. (3 marks)
5 Explain what red means on a traffic light label. (2 marks)

4.4 Common types of food poisoning

Food poisoning can be caused by pathogenic bacteria but it can also be caused by viruses, chemicals and metals contaminating the food. Food can even be contaminated with poisonous plants and animals.

Figure 4.11 **Rats carry pathogenic bacteria that can lead to food poisoning**

Table 4.2 **Common types of food poisoning**

Pathogenic bacteria	Source	Special points
Campylobacter	Raw meat, raw poultry, animal contamination, milk and milk products Found in the intestines of many types of animals and birds; birds can contaminate food by pecking it and with their droppings Inadequately pasteurised milk and contaminated water supplies are responsible for larger outbreaks of the disease	The most common form of bacterial food poisoning in the UK Less than 500 *Campylobacter* bacteria are needed to cause infection Destroyed by heat
Salmonella	Eggs, poultry, cooked meats, unpasteurised milk, insects and sewage Found in the intestines of farm animals and sometimes human beings Pets and rodents can carry the bacteria	As *Salmonella* is infectious (it can be passed from person to person easily) make sure the toilet areas and personal bedding are kept clean Avoid drinking water from untreated sources It is destroyed by cooking
Escherichia coli (*E. coli*)	Raw and undercooked meats; raw poultry; untreated milk, water and dairy products Found in the intestines of animals and humans	Only a small number of bacteria can produce sufficient toxin to cause an illness The bacteria can survive refrigeration and freezer storage Thorough cooking of food and pasteurisation will destroy it ➡

Table 4.2 Common types of food poisoning (continued)

Pathogenic bacteria	Source	Special points
Clostridium perfringens	Healthy animals and people, raw meat, soil from root vegetables, dust and animal excreta, sewage, manure	Can occur when food, usually meat, is prepared in advance and kept warm for several hours before serving *Clostridium perfringens* can reproduce during slow cooling and unrefrigerated storage **Spores** develop in the danger zone and anaerobic conditions Spores can survive low temperatures When consumed it produces a toxin that causes illness
Listeria	Cook chilled foods (foods that have been cooked and then chilled and stored in the fridge), for example ready meals Untreated dairy foods, pâté, smoked fish, soil, sewage, water, animals and people	It can grow at low temperatures and will multiply in refrigerators at 5°C It is destroyed by cooking food thoroughly and by the process of pasteurisation Pregnant women, babies, those with a weakened immune system and the elderly are most at risk Infections during pregnancy can cause miscarriage or premature delivery Vulnerable groups should avoid eating unpasteurised dairy products Salads and raw vegetables should be washed before eating
Bacillus cereus	Cooked rice and pasta dishes, meat and vegetable dishes, dairy products, soups, sauces, sweet pastry products, cereals and cereal products, dust and soil Usually these food products have not been cooled or stored correctly; food that has been inadequately reheated can also be the source	During cooling time after cooking, the spores will produce bacteria; bacteria can multiply rapidly at these warm temperatures and produce heat-resistant toxins that are not destroyed by further reheating Only a small number of bacteria are required to cause illness
Staphylococcus aureus	Raw milk, meat and meat products The human body – *Staphylococcus aureus* can live on the skin, in the nose or on the fingers of some infected people	Cross-contamination occurs when an infected person handles ready-to-eat foods; storage of infected foods at room temperature before consumption allows the bacteria to multiply and produce a harmful toxin High standards of personal hygiene are essential Most strains of *Staphylococcus aureus* are destroyed effectively by antibiotics but some are resistant to the antibiotic methicillin – they are known as methicillin-resistant *Staphylococcus aureus* (MRSA)

Spore: dormant form of bacteria able to survive when conditions are not perfect, e.g. there is not enough water or the temperature is too hot or cold. When conditions improve, spores can produce more bacteria.

Sources of food poisoning

Food can become contaminated during production, preparation and retailing. The main sources are:

- raw food – for example meat, poultry, shellfish and eggs
- people – food-poisoning bacteria are found on the skin, in septic wounds, in the nose and sometimes in the gut
- pests – for example rats, mice, cockroaches, ants, wasps and flies
- animals – domestic pets and farm animals can carry *E. coli* in their intestines
- air and dust – food must be covered as bacteria in the air can settle on the surface
- water – bacteria such as *Salmonella* are carried in untreated water
- soil – bacteria and spores can survive in soil, so can be found on unwashed root vegetables
- food waste – waste needs to be disposed of correctly as it could be a source of contamination and may attract pests.

Conditions necessary for food poisoning

Bacteria can grow rapidly in the correct conditions. A single **bacterium** can divide into two by a process called **binary fission**. A single bacterium can produce 16 million bacteria in only twelve hours.

Food-poisoning bacteria have four essential requirements for growth:

- **Food** – bacteria grow rapidly in high-risk foods that are good sources of protein, such as cooked meat and poultry, shellfish and seafood, uncooked or lightly cooked eggs, unpasteurised milk and cheeses, cooked rice and pasta, and salads.
- **Moisture** – bacteria cannot multiply without moisture, which means that they do not usually affect dried foods or products with high quantities of sugar and salt, which absorb water.
- **Warmth** – most bacteria multiply at **ambient temperature** – normal room temperature. This falls within the danger zone between 5 °C and 63 °C. Below 5 °C most bacteria are unable to multiply rapidly, and below −18 °C they become **dormant**. Cooking food at temperatures above 63 °C will destroy most bacteria; when cooked, the food should reach 75 °C for at least two minutes.
- **Time** – in the right conditions the number of bacteria can double every 20 minutes.

The acidity or alkalinity of a food also influences the growth of bacteria. If conditions are too acidic or too alkaline, bacteria cannot grow.

> **Bacterium**: a single bacteria.
>
> **Binary fission**: the process by which bacteria reproduce by splitting into two.
>
> **Ambient temperature**: normal room temperature.
>
> **Dormant**: a period of inactivity when bacteria are unable to multiply.

Revision activity

Make revision cards on each bacteria – use information from this chapter and the next chapter to have as much information as you can on each one.

Figure 4.12 **Prawn cocktail is a high-risk food**

Exam tip

You need to know the names of the different food poisoning bacteria along with their sources. In the next chapter you will also learn the onset time, symptoms and how long the symptoms will last.

Typical mistake

You may be asked to name some high-risk foods. A common mistake is to write about sources of food-poisoning bacteria such as raw meat or poultry instead. High-risk foods are ready-to-eat foods that can support the growth of food-poisoning bacteria – correct answers would include cooked meat or poultry, homemade mayonnaise and cooked rice.

Now test yourself

TESTED

1 Name four sources of bacteria. (4 marks)
2 What are the essential requirements for food-poisoning bacteria to grow? (2 marks)
3 What temperature is the 'danger zone'? (1 mark)
4 Which food-poisoning bacteria can cause miscarriage or premature delivery? (1 mark)
5 Which food-poisoning bacteria is found in the human body? (1 mark)

4.5 Symptoms of food-induced ill health

How bacteria make you ill

REVISED

- **Eating pathogenic bacteria** – when bacteria enter the stomach and intestine they multiply. This is how *Campylobacter* and *Salmonella* cause illness. Some types of food poisoning require the consumption of thousands of bacteria; others, such as *E. coli*, only require the consumption of a few to cause serious illness.
- **Eating a toxin** – a toxin is a poison produced as a waste product by bacteria. Some bacteria, such as *Staphylococcus aureus* and *Bacillus cereus*, produce a toxin when they multiply. Eating the toxin makes you ill, not eating the bacteria.

Symptoms of food poisoning

REVISED

- A symptom is a sign or indication of a disease.
- The body reacts to bacteria or toxins by developing symptoms such as diarrhoea, vomiting, stomach pain, headaches and sweating.
- Some of these symptoms are visible and some are non-visible.

Table 4.3 Visible and non-visible symptoms of food poisoning

Visible symptoms	Non-visible symptoms
Shivering	Feeling tired or weak
Diarrhoea	Stomach ache
Vomiting	Headache
	Feeling nauseous (sick)

- Food poisoning usually begins shortly after eating the contaminated source. The **onset time** is the period of time between eating the contaminated food and the symptoms of food poisoning appearing.
- The onset time is much shorter in bacteria that produce toxins – these symptoms can appear within a few hours.

> **Onset time**: the time it takes for the symptoms of food poisoning to appear after eating contaminated food.

Table 4.4 Onset times and typical symptoms of common types of food poisoning

Pathogenic bacteria	Average onset time and duration of symptoms	Typical symptoms
Campylobacter	2–5 days after infection Usually lasts a week	Diarrhoea, vomiting, stomach pains and cramps, fever, generally feeling unwell
Salmonella	12–72 hours after infection Usually lasts 4–7 days	Abdominal pain, diarrhoea, vomiting, headache and high fever *Salmonella* causes dehydration and this can be particularly serious in young children, the sick and the elderly. Fatalities (deaths) from the disease are rare
E. coli	2 days Usually lasts 3–10 days	Abdominal pain, nausea, mild diarrhoea, bloody diarrhoea due to severe inflammation of the gut, vomiting, kidney failure Can be fatal
Clostridium perfringens	Within hours of consuming the bacteria Usually lasts 24–48 hours	Abdominal pain, diarrhoea, nausea
Listeria	Can take up 90 days for symptoms to appear, so identifying the source of infection can be a challenge Usually lasts a few days, but can last up to 2–3 weeks	Mild flu to serious complications – blood poisoning or meningitis Gastroenteritis Can cause miscarriage
Bacillus cereus	1–16 hours after infection Usually lasts 24–48 hours	Nausea, vomiting
Staphylococcus aureus	1–6 hours after infection Usually lasts 1–3 days	Abdominal pain, severe vomiting, low temperature, diarrhoea, stomach pain Can cause blood and wound infections if there is an opportunity for the bacteria to enter the body

Symptoms of food allergies

A food allergy is a serious reaction to a food or ingredients in food. It is caused by the body's immune system reacting to an allergen. If the reaction to a food is a bad one, it could give the following symptoms:

- skin rash
- itchiness of skin, eyes and mouth
- swollen lips, face, eyes
- difficulties in breathing.

In severe cases, it can bring about **anaphylactic shock** – the person develops swelling in their throat and mouth, making it difficult to speak or breathe. This can lead to death if appropriate treatment, such as an EpiPen, is not used quickly.

Figure 4.13 **A skin rash can be a reaction to an allergen**

> **Anaphylactic shock**: a severe allergic reaction that can be fatal.

Symptoms of food intolerances and coeliac disease

Some people have a sensitivity to certain foods, which can cause symptoms such as nausea, abdominal pain, joint aches and pains, tiredness and weakness. This is called a food intolerance – this is not an allergic reaction and it does not involve the immune system.

Coeliac disease is neither a food allergy nor a food intolerance but an autoimmune disease caused by a reaction of the immune system to gluten – a protein found in wheat, rye and barley. The symptoms of coeliac disease vary from person to person and can range from very mild to severe.

Symptoms of coeliac disease include:

- severe diarrhoea, excessive wind and/or constipation
- persistent or unexplained gastrointestinal symptoms, such as nausea and vomiting
- recurrent stomach pain, cramping or bloating
- iron, vitamin B12 or folic acid deficiency
- anaemia
- tiredness
- sudden or unexpected weight loss.

The only treatment for coeliac disease is a gluten free diet for life. Even very small amounts of gluten can be damaging to people with coeliac disease; therefore taking steps to avoid cross contamination with gluten is important. Only foods that contain 20 parts per million (ppm) or less can be labelled as 'gluten free'.

Look out for the Coeliac UK GF symbol in catering venues. The trademarked GF Symbol can only be used by caterers who have been awarded with GF accreditation by the charity Coeliac UK to clearly demonstrate their competency and commitment to the preparation and service of gluten free food.

Symptoms of lactose intolerance include:

- abdominal pain
- nausea
- diarrhoea
- flatulence.

Figure 4.14 **Coeliacs should look for this sign on a menu, which tells them the food is gluten free**

Revision activity

Create a revision table on the symptoms of food intolerances, allergies and pathogenic bacteria. Note which are the visible symptoms and which are the non-visible symptoms.

Exam tip

This section has a lot of facts and figures – you need to learn them.

Typical mistake

If you have not learned your facts and figures for this section then you are likely to get the answer wrong and lose valuable marks.

Now test yourself

TESTED

1 Name three symptoms of coeliac disease.   (3 marks)
2 Name two symptoms of a person who is lactose intolerant and has eaten a dairy product.   (2 marks)
3 Explain how bacteria can make you ill.   (2 marks)
4 Name three visible symptoms of food poisoning.   (3 marks)
5 What is the onset time of *Salmonella* and how long do the symptoms last? (2 marks)

Unit 1 LO5 Be able to propose a hospitality and catering provision to meet specific requirements

5.1 & 5.2 Options for hospitality and catering provision

- In Learning objective 1, Understand the environment in which hospitality and catering providers operate, starting on page 6, you learned that the hospitality and catering industry provides accommodation, and food and drinks, in venues outside of the home.
- The providers of hospitality and catering offer a wide variety of options for visitors with specific needs and for different locations and situations.
- Tables 5.1 and 5.2 show a number of different options for catering and accommodation, along with their advantages and disadvantages.

Catering options

REVISED

Table 5.1 **Advantages and disadvantages of different catering options**

Provision	Advantages	Disadvantages
Restaurants and **bistros**	Waiter service Can ask questions about the menu Comfortable seating at a table	Often more expensive than other options Waiting time can be longer than other options
Pop-up restaurants	Often set up in convenient locations Prices can be cheaper Gives customers a chance to try new foods	The menu may be limited Only in location for a limited time
Cafe	Faster service than a restaurant Lower prices than a restaurant Wide menu choices – something for everyone	Can be crowded Seating may not be very comfortable, for example **fixed seats**

Bistro: a small, relaxed French-style restaurant; prices are generally cheaper than a restaurant.

Fixed seats: seating that is permanently fixed to the floor.

Table 5.1 Advantages and disadvantages of different catering options (continued)

Provision	Advantages	Disadvantages
Street food	Usually fast service Cheap prices Food is wrapped and ready to go Can ask questions about ingredients etc.	Hygiene may not be as good as indoor venues, for example lack of pest control and temperature control There may be no seating available Usually need cash to pay
Mobile vans	Serve fresh, hot food Very convenient if in your location	Only available at set days/times Limited menu choice Engine fumes can be a problem if engine left running
Fast food	Fast service Fast cooking, as food is often prepared/cooked beforehand Cheaper prices Easy to eat	Often unhealthy choices Not all packaging can be **recycled** so may be damaging for the environment
Takeaways and **drive-throughs**	Fast and convenient Cheaper prices No need to get out of the car at drive-throughs, so convenient for families with children and disabled customers	Menu choice is limited Often unhealthy choices
Tearooms and coffee shops	Service is usually fast Food is often freshly prepared Good for snacks and lighter meals Branded coffee shops offer a familiar setting and menu	Limited menu choice Can be crowded Seating may not be comfortable, for example raised stools Can be expensive
Delicatessens and salad bars	Offer a wide range of salads and sandwiches Often sell hot food such as soups and jacket potatoes	Waiting times can be long at peak times as food is often made to order Seating may be limited or in a small space
Pubs and bars	Food often available all day Generous portion sizes Wide menu choices Prices often cheaper than restaurants Comfortable atmosphere	Seating may not be comfortable, for example raised stools Waiting time can be longer than some other options, for example fast food and cafes

Recycled: converting waste products into reusable material.

Drive-throughs: type of service that allows customers to purchase products without leaving their cars.

Table 5.1 Advantages and disadvantages of different catering options (continued)

Provision	Advantages	Disadvantages
Private clubs and casinos	Friendly service Lots of staff available to help Offer various food and drink choices	Membership is often required for private clubs, which can be expensive Menu choices can be limited There may be a dress code, for example men may need to wear a shirt and tie
Visitor attractions (for example theme parks)	Catering sited in convenient locations Fast service Choice of catering options to suit different guests May offer meal deals or unlimited drinks	The food is often expensive Can be long queues Small portions Some visitor attractions don't allow you to take your own food in, so they have a **captive market**
Sport and concert stadiums	Convenient Fast service Easy to eat foods	Long queues Often expensive Often no seating available Limited menu
Vending machine	Very convenient Open 24/7 Some take card payments	Choice of food/drinks very limited Can be expensive Machines may only take cash Can be **out of order** or money lost with no one around to help

Captive market: markets in which consumers can only choose between a limited number of suppliers; their only choice is to purchase what is available or to make no purchase at all.

Out of order: not working correctly or not working at all.

Figure 5.1 Cafe

Figure 5.2 Drive-through

Figure 5.3 Salad bar

Figure 5.4 Pubs and bars

Figure 5.5 Vending machine

Table 5.2 Advantages and disadvantages of different accommodation options

Provision	Advantages	Disadvantages
Youth and backpacker hostels	Cater for single people, couples, families and groups travelling on a limited budget Basic but wholesome meals are provided Self-catering facilities are usually available Some rooms are private and have en suite bathrooms Open to all ages	Mainly **dormitory accommodation** May have to share bedroom/bathroom with others Food choice is very limited Usually pay more if you are not a member
Holiday parks	Suitable for single people, families and groups Offer a wide variety of activities for all ages Activities are scheduled at different times of the day to allow forward planning and choice Facilities for guests with limited mobility levels are usually very good Kids clubs are available which allow families time apart to follow their own interests	Can be expensive Quality of food and the food choices may be limited Lack of privacy Can be a noisy environment
B&Bs and guest houses	Often small and family run Friendly service Good value for money Guest houses may offer lunch and an evening meal	Less privacy than a hotel May have to share bathroom facilities with other guests
Farmhouses	Often offer B&B and holiday cottages Bedrooms meet national tourist board standards Rooms are inspected to make sure they offer value and quality	Some farms can be noisy and/or smelly depending on the type of farm Animals may wake up early, especially in the summer, which can disturb guests
Budget hotels (for example Travelodge, Premier Inn)	Cheaper than regular hotels Convenient locations, for example near motorways and airports Tea- and coffee-making facilities available Shops, cafes and restaurants close by Many have Wi-Fi	Few staff on duty at any one time Can be noisy if near a motorway or airport Some restaurants are located next door to budget hotels, rather than as part of the hotel
Luxury hotels	Offer room service Have Wi-Fi Often have sports facilities, such as a gym or swimming pool May have office and IT services Provide food 24/7 Have a choice of eating venues	Expensive Dress code may be formal

Table 5.2 Advantages and disadvantages of different accommodation options (continued)

Provision	Advantages	Disadvantages
Boutique hotel	Friendly service Relaxed atmosphere Very suitable for couples Reputation for good food and wine	Expensive Children may not be allowed

Figure 5.7 **Youth hostel**

> **Dormitory accommodation**: a large sleeping room containing several beds.

Figure 5.6 **Budget hotel**   Figure 5.8 **Luxury hotel**

Proposing ideas

REVISED

In the Unit 1 assessment, you will need to be able to match different types of visitors to suitable types of catering and/or accommodation. The different types of visitors could include:

- families with children under 12
- families with teenage children
- groups of people, for example a school group
- old age pensioners (OAPs)
- overseas visitors
- single people
- couples.

A range of information must be gathered to be able to make a structured proposal for catering and accommodation for a specific requirement. You need to consider factors such as:

- budget available
- type of occasion
- type of venue
- number of people in the group
- information about the area.

The information given in the question should be used in your answer. Make sure you try to cover all the points made in the question to get more marks.

Justifying your decisions

You need to be able to review (go over) and justify (say why) the reasons for the options you have chosen. For high marks you will need to be very clear and give as much detail as you can about the catering and/or accommodation selected.

You should select and reject different catering and accommodation options, and give clear reasons why you have accepted or rejected them.

The key points you make should be closely linked to the question and the scenario set.

Example 1

Jacob is a single student on a low income who needs a meal and somewhere to stay for the night.

Answer

Jacob may decide to buy street food when eating out of the home, as it is good value and very convenient.

The least likely provision for Jacob would be a restaurant, as this would be too expensive and he may feel uncomfortable eating at a table on his own.

Jacob may decide to stay in a youth hostel as he will have the company of others and it is less expensive than other options. The least likely provision would be a luxury hotel, as this would be too expensive and his appearance/clothes may not be smart enough for a luxury hotel environment.

Example 2

Vivian and Sharif are a couple on a high income.

Answer

Vivian and Sharif may decide to eat out at a restaurant as they would be prepared to pay more for better service and high-quality food. The least likely provision would be a vending machine as the selection of food is very limited, often just snacks rather than a meal.

Vivian and Sharif may decide to stay in a boutique hotel as it would provide a quieter environment with more privacy and time to relax. The least likely provision would be a youth hostel as they generally offer shared facilities and often have single-gender dormitories, meaning that Vivian and Sharif would be separated overnight.

Using supporting information

For the Unit 1 assessment, you will be given information in the question that you need to refer to in your answer. This information may include:

- the type of visitors, for example families or groups
- the type of venue, for example a theme park
- the budget of the visitors, for example on a medium budget where the family can afford one meal at the theme park but snacks and drinks need to be brought in from home

- food provision needed, for example lunch, snacks and drinks only
- accommodation provision needed, for example a budget hotel
- information about the area, for example a seaside town with lots of cafes and some B&B accommodation available.

You should refer to this information in your answer to show that you have met the needs of the visitor group and their specific requirements as stated in the question.

Typical mistake

Some students do not achieve high marks when answering exam questions as they are very general in their responses and do not give specific examples for the choice of catering or accommodation options.

High marks can only be achieved with clear and detailed explanations about why particular catering and accommodation options have been chosen, based on the information given in the question.

Now test yourself

TESTED ☐

1 State two advantages and two disadvantages of buying street food. (4 marks)
2 State two advantages and two disadvantages of staying in a budget hotel. (4 marks)
3 Identify four examples of different types of visitors who may use both catering and accommodation facilities. (4 marks)
4 Select two types of accommodation for old age pensioners (OAPs) on a low income. Give reasons why this accommodation is suitable. (4 marks)
5 Discuss why holiday parks provide a good choice of food for families. Give two different catering options likely to be on offer at a holiday park. (4 marks)

Revision activity

Make some revision flash cards. On one side write a provision for catering (for example takeaway food); on the other side write one advantage and one disadvantage of each catering provider (for example: advantage – fast and convenient, disadvantage – often unhealthy choices). Repeat this for the provision of accommodation. Learn one advantage and one disadvantage of each provider.

Exam tip

Read the question carefully. Is it asking about catering or accommodation options, or both? Once you know this you can match the visitor type to suitable catering and/or accommodation options.

LO5 Be able to propose a hospitality and catering provision to meet specific requirements

Exam practice

1 What is the main role of a head chef?
   a) Be in charge of the kitchen brigade.
   b) Cook all the meals.
   c) Look after the desserts section.
   d) Prepare the fruit and vegetables. [1]
2 Describe the role of a sous chef. [4]
3 Many hotels have conference facilities.
   a) State **two** groups of people that may use these facilities. [2]
   b) Identify **three** different facilities they may need during the conference. [3]
4 Some people attending the conference may need overnight accommodation. State two advantages to the hotel and two advantages to the person staying overnight. [4]
5 Discuss the health and safety issues that would need to be considered when planning an event at a hotel where food and drink would be served. [8]
6 Explain how the microbes yeasts and moulds can spoil food. [6]
7 Describe the role of an Environmental Health Officer (EHO). [6]
8 Discuss one advantage and one disadvantage of each of the following catering options for students on a low income:
   a) Street food [2]
   b) Casino [2]
   c) Vending machine [2]
9 Suggest, with reasons, one type of accommodation that an elderly couple on a high income may choose for a short break. [6]

ONLINE

Answers and quick quizzes at **www.hoddereducation.co.uk/myrevisionnotes**

Success in the examination

For Unit 1 of the WJEC Level 1/2 Vocational Award in Hospitality and Catering you will complete an assessment under exam conditions.

You are likely to be asked to complete this assessment on a computer – this is called an **e-assessment**. Some schools may complete a paper version of the assessment. Your teacher will tell you how you will complete the assessment in advance.

- You will have one hour and 30 minutes to complete the assessment.
- There will be 90 marks available for the exam.
- The assessment will include a mixture of short- and extended-answer questions. You need to answer **all** of the questions.

Tips on preparing for the exam

REVISED

- Always ask your teacher if you don't understand something. There is no such thing as a stupid question. Your teacher is there to help you.
- It is never too early to start revising. After each lesson, read your lesson notes and handouts, then make concise revision notes for each topic. The more times you revise a topic, the better you will perform in the exam.

Approaching the paper

REVISED

- You should read the instructions on the first page; these are your instructions for answering the questions.
- Read each question twice to make sure you understand what to do.
- Check how many marks are available for each question. This will tell you how much detail to give in your answers. For example, if there are six marks you may need to give six answers, or you may give three answers and give a reason or explanation for each one.
- When you go through the questions for the first time, just answer the questions you find easy. If a question seems tricky and you are not sure what to do, leave it and go on to the next question. The second time you go through the questions, answer the ones you are fairly confident with. On the third attempt, have a go at answering the trickier questions. Finally, attempt the questions you find very difficult. You should not leave any questions unanswered. A blank space never gets a mark, but sometimes a good guess does!
- Have a positive attitude. Do not allow self-doubt to affect your preparation or success.

Success in the examination

Assess	Give your informed judgement on something; put a value on it; judge the worth of something
	Example: Assess the factors that may contribute to the risk of food poisoning when handling raw chicken.
Compare	Point out the differences and similarities between the given items
	Example: Compare a one-star hotel with a five-star hotel.
Consider	Think about something in order to understand it or make a decision
	Example: Consider which types of large kitchen equipment are important in a commercial kitchen.
Contrast	Point out the differences between two or more given items
	Example: Contrast a blast chiller and a refrigerator.
Describe	Write out the main features; write a picture in words
	Example: Describe the main features of a five-star hotel.
Discuss	Write from more than one viewpoint, supporting and casting doubt; it is not always necessary to come to a conclusion
	Example: Discuss how leftover food may be safely used in meal preparation.
Draw conclusions from	Explain what you learned
	Example: Draw conclusions from the food safety documentation.
Evaluate	Judge the worth of something; sum up the good and bad parts, and decide how improvements may be made
	Example: Evaluate the staff allocation in your local fast-food restaurant.
Explain	Set out the facts and the reasons for them, make them known in detail and make them plain and clear
	Example: Explain why raw and cooked meat should be kept apart.
Identify	Describe what someone or something is
	Example: Identify two types of food service.
Justify	Give adequate grounds for decisions or conclusions; prove to be right; give a good reason
	Example: Justify why you have chosen this menu for young children.
Outline	Write out the main points or a general plan, but omit minor details
	Example: Outline the main factors that affect the choice of accommodation for families.
Select	Carefully choose as being the best or most suitable
	Example: Select one type of hospitality and catering provision to meet the needs of young children.
State	Give only the bare facts, clearly and fully
	Example: State the types of visitors most likely to visit a youth hostel.
Suggest	Make a recommendation or suggestion
	Example: Suggest three different hospitality and catering training courses suitable for school leavers.

Sample examination questions and model answers

Stimulus questions

In some questions you will you will be provided with a photograph or diagram and will be asked to answer questions in relation to the image. You may be asked to match the image with a correct description or to place it in the correct category.

> **Example**
>
> 1 Identify the equipment below which is used in a commercial kitchen. (3 marks)
>
> a)  b)  c)
>
> *Candidate response*
>
> a) Induction hob
>
> b) Deep-fat fryer
>
> c) Large mixer
>
> *Assessment comment*
>
> The candidate has identified all pieces of equipment correctly – award three marks.

Short-answer questions

These questions are likely to ask you to **identify**, **state**, **describe** or **explain** something. They may be based around an example scenario from the hospitality and catering industry. They tend to be worth between one and six marks.

> **Example**
>
> 2 Identify who is in charge of choosing and serving wine in a fine dining restaurant. (1 mark)
>
> *Candidate response*
>
> Sommelier
>
> *Assessment comment*
>
> This answer is correct.

Data response questions

These questions are likely to provide you with a table of data, chart, pie chart or graph, and ask you to answer questions based on the data provided and your own understanding of the topic.

Example

3   The following chart shows the percentage of food wastage in the restaurant industry (source: WRAP, www.wrap.org.uk). State four ways in which a restaurant can reduce food wastage.

(4 marks)

Candidate response

Food that is left over can be reused to make another dish.

Always checking stock to make sure the oldest items are used first.

Making sure that customers have the right sized portion – not too big.

Give them a 'doggy bag' to take uneaten food home.

Assessment comment

The candidate has correctly stated four ways in which a restaurant can reduce waste – award four marks.

Example

4   Star Theme Park is set in 800 acres and located in the North of England with good road and public transport links. The theme park includes several roller coasters and a water park. Most rides are aimed at older children and adults who enjoy the thrill of big rides.

Star Theme Park has decided that it would like to provide overnight accommodation for its visitors to encourage them to stay longer than one day.

The following chart shows the percentage of visitors of different types at Star Theme Park.

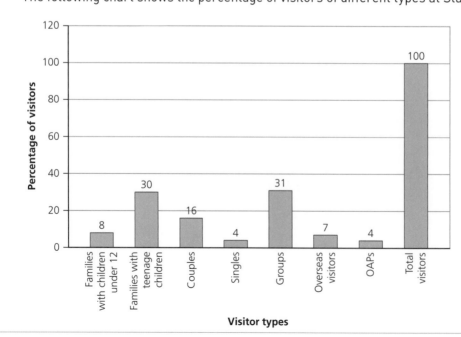

a) Suggest two types of accommodation that meet the needs of visitors to Star Theme Park.

(2 marks)

b) Review your two accommodation suggestions and evaluate which one is the most suitable to meet the needs of visitors to the theme park.

(9 marks)

Mark scheme

Level 1	Outlines in general the proposed idea for accommodation provision with some basic reasoning for choice. There will be some evidence of structuring information.	Award 1–3 marks
Level 2 Pass	Outlines detailed reasons for the choice of accommodation provision at Star Theme Park. Learners will have used data from the chart to evaluate decisions relating to the needs of the visitors. Options are communicated in a logical structure and learners have attempted to use appropriate tone and style. Use of the chart of the types of visitors to the theme park would be used to validate the provision to meet the needs of the visitors.	Award 4–6 marks
Level 2 Merit	In-depth explanation for the reasons for choice of the accommodation is given. This is based on information from the bar chart. Evidence contains detailed reasons of how the provision would meet the needs of the visitors to Star Theme Park. The style will be clear and logical, using appropriate tone and style of language. Selection and rejection of the two types of accommodation would be evident with good reasoning.	Award 7–9 marks

Candidate response A

a) A hostel and a budget hotel

b) A hostel provides cheaper accommodation than other options. It is a sociable type of accommodation and will provide somewhere to sleep and a simple breakfast. Some hostels also provide packed lunches and evening meals, as well as self-catering facilities. The accommodation is basic but it could be ideal for groups of people (which make up 31 per cent of visitors – the largest group) as a whole section of the hostel could be rented out. This would provide a secure and cheap option, especially for groups, which are one of the main types of visitors to the theme park. In addition, many YHA (Youth Hostel Association) hostels provide family rooms and some even have en suite facilities.

A budget hotel offers en suite rooms that usually sleep up to four people and are very good value for money. If they are booked in advance, the prices can be even cheaper. Although the hotel won't have leisure amenities such as games rooms or swimming pools, these won't be needed as visitors will be out of the hotel at the theme park for most of the day. Some budget hotels don't have restaurants/shops on site, but these are usually close by for meals and other essentials, which is important for families (which make up 38 per cent of visitors in total). Budget hotels such as Premier Inn and Travelodge are in many towns and cities across the UK; there are hundreds of these hotels. A budget hotel would be suitable for almost all of the visitor types who don't mind having a basic hotel room with limited facilities.

Summing up, I would choose a budget hotel for visitors to the theme park. As most provide en-suite facilities and towels, it would be very convenient for some groups, most families and couples. Although these hotels may not be suitable for all groups, this would depend on their age, as budget hotels normally require each room to be occupied by at least one adult.

Assessment comment

The response is thorough and meets all the assessment criteria needed for top band marks – Level 2 Merit. Award two marks for section A and nine marks for section B.

Candidate response B

a) A luxury hotel and a budget hotel

b) I have chosen a budget hotel for the visitors to the theme park as the chart shows that there are lots of different types of visitors to the park. This accommodation would be ideal as it would meet the needs of families and couples. As it's a budget hotel, it would be affordable for most types of visitors. It should be OK for the 31 per cent of visitors that are groups, but this depends on the age of everyone. At some budget hotels only two or sometimes three adults are allowed to share the same room.

Assessment comment

Generally, any commercial accommodation is acceptable for answers of these types, but it would need to be justified in section B. For section B the response outlines reasons for choice of the budget hotel, but not in great depth. The luxury hotel is not mentioned. Level 2 Pass – award two marks for section A and five marks for section B.

Extended-answer questions

REVISED

Extended-answer questions are likely to ask you to write in more detail. They may ask you to analyse, provide examples, review options and make recommendations. They are likely to be worth more marks.

These questions tend to be marked based on the level of your response.

Example

5 Explain why customer care in a hotel is important.　　　(9 marks)

Mark scheme

Level 1	Explains in general why customer care is important. There will be some evidence of structuring information.	Award 1–3 marks
Level 2 Pass	Explains in detail why customer care is important. Explanations are communicated in a logical structure and attempt to use appropriate tone and style.	Award 4–6 marks
Level 2 Merit	In-depth explanation why customer care is important. The style will be clear and logical, using appropriate tone and style of language.	Award 7–9 marks

➡

Candidate response

Good customer care will mean that people are more likely to return because they have had a good experience. They could also tell other people how good the hotel was and that they would come again. This is really good advertising for the business as it would mean more customers returning, and potentially new customers, which would make more money for the business by increasing profits.

On the other hand, if a business does not provide good customer care, the hotel may get a bad reputation.

Assessment comment

They began the answer well with one good explanation of why customer care is important; the second explanation is correct but needs more detail for a higher mark. If they had also explained one or two more points, they would have achieved a higher mark Level 1 pass – award three marks.

Unit 2 LO1 Understand the importance of nutrition when planning menus

1.1 Functions of nutrients in the human body

Food provides the nutrients and energy that the body needs for growth, repair and maintenance so that it can stay healthy and work properly.

There are five nutrient groups: protein, fats, carbohydrates, vitamins and minerals.

Water and dietary fibre (also known as NSP) are often included with the nutrients. Although they are not nutrients, they are essential in a healthy diet.

Protein

- Protein is needed for growth, repair and general maintenance of the body.
- Proteins are made up of **amino acids**. There are ten essential amino acids.
- **High biological value (HBV) proteins** contain all of the essential amino acids; meat, fish, eggs, cheese and soybeans are examples of HBV proteins.
- **Low biological value (LBV) proteins** are missing one or more of the essential amino acids; beans, peas, lentils, nuts and cereals are examples of LBV proteins.

> **Amino acids:** the building blocks of proteins.
>
> **High biological value (HBV) proteins:** proteins that contain all ten essential amino acids, for example eggs and fish.
>
> **Low biological value (LBV) proteins:** proteins that lack one or more of the ten essential amino acids, for example nuts and lentils.

Table 6.1 **Animal and vegetable sources of protein**

Animal sources of protein	Vegetable sources of protein
Meat, poultry, fish, eggs, offal, cheese, milk	Beans, peas, lentils, cereal grains, nuts, Quorn, tofu, quinoa, seeds

Fats

- Fats are an important source of energy and they also insulate the body.
- Fats are solid at room temperature; oils are liquid at room temperature.
- Some fats you can see, for example butter, lard and suet. Some fats you can't see, for example the fat in cheese or cakes.
- Animal fats include butter, lard, meats, oily fish, hard cheese and cream.
- Oils such as sunflower and olive, nuts and nut products (for example, peanut butter) and seeds (for example, sesame seeds) are vegetable fats.

Carbohydrates

- Carbohydrates are the main energy source for the body.
- They may come from **sugary foods** such as cakes, sweets and biscuits, as well as from **starchy foods** such as bread, rice, pasta and potatoes.

> **Sugary foods**: foods that contain a large amount of refined sugar, for example biscuits, cakes and sweets.
>
> **Starchy foods**: foods that contain a large amount of starch, for example bread, rice, pasta and potatoes.

Vitamins

Vitamins are responsible for controlling many chemical reactions in the body.

Table 6.2 **Sources of vitamins and what they do**

Vitamin	Main food sources	What the nutrient does in the body
Vitamin A	Eggs, oily fish, liver, whole milk, spinach, carrots, sweet potatoes, mangoes, apricots	Helps sight in poor light and strengthens the immune system Needed for healthy skin and mucous membranes
B group vitamins	Bread, eggs, meat, chicken, milk, potatoes	Keeps the skin, eyes and nervous system healthy Needed to release energy from food
Vitamin C	Fruits and vegetables, especially oranges, blackcurrants, broccoli, strawberries and red peppers	Helps the body to absorb iron Keeps body cells healthy and helps the healing process
Vitamin D	Whole milk, butter, oily fish, eggs, fortified breakfast cereals, fat spreads	Helps the body absorb the minerals needed for healthy bones – calcium and phosphorus
Vitamin E	Seeds, nuts, vegetable oils, wholegrain foods	Helps to prevent cancer and heart disease as it is an antioxidant
Vitamin K	Green leafy vegetables such as cabbage and spring greens; meat and liver	Needed for normal clotting of the blood

Minerals

Minerals control many chemical processes and maintain fluid balances in the body.

Table 6.3 **Sources of minerals and what they do**

Mineral	Main food sources	What the nutrient does in the body
Calcium	Nuts, bread and fortified cereals, cheese, milk, green leafy vegetables, oily fish, soya and tofu	Builds strong bones and teeth Controls muscle function and heartbeat Helps blood clotting
Iron	Red meat, cabbage, kale, lentils, tofu, quinoa, egg yolks	Makes the haemoglobin in red blood cells that carries oxygen around the body
Sodium	Salt, cheese, bacon, bread, smoked fish, ready meals, salted nuts	Essential to balance fluids in the body, such as blood Excess sodium leads to high blood pressure, strokes and heart attacks

Water

- Water is essential for the survival of the human body.
- It cools the body by sweating, to prevent cell damage and overheating.
- It transports waste products from the body.
- Most people need about 2 litres of water a day (about eight average-size glasses). Water can also be found in soft drinks, milk, fruit juices and drinks made with water, such as tea, coffee and squash.
- **Dehydration** occurs when your body loses more water than you take in.

> **Dehydration**: when your body loses more water than you take in.

Dietary fibre (NSP)

- **Fibre** is a type of indigestible carbohydrate that is found in fruits, vegetables and wholegrain foods, such as wholemeal bread and brown rice.
- Fibre is needed to help the body get rid of waste (faeces).
- Dietary fibre is also called non-starch polysaccharides (NSP) fibre.

> **Fibre**: a type of indigestible carbohydrate needed to help the body get rid of waste.

Assessment tip

To get a high mark in your internal assessment you need to describe clearly the functions of a range of nutrients, water and dietary fibre in the human body. You could present this work in a table or in separate paragraphs. It needs to be clear and accurate, for example:
- *Protein – needed for growth, repair and general maintenance of the body.*
- *Fats – an important source of energy; they also insulate the body.*
- *Carbohydrates – the main energy source for the body.*
- *Vitamin A – helps sight in poor light and strengthens the immune system; needed for healthy skin and mucous membranes.*
- *Calcium – builds strong bones and teeth, controls muscle function and heartbeat, and helps blood clotting.*

Figure 6.1 Bran flakes are a good source of dietary fibre

Typical mistake

Students sometimes only mention protein, fats and carbohydrates when describing the functions of nutrients. The full range of nutrients, including individual vitamins and minerals, should be clearly described to gain the highest mark for this assessment criterion.

Revision activity

Make a mind map for each nutrient. Write the name of the nutrient in the middle and then note around it the foods that contain it. Add the function(s) of this nutrient by including some sketches around the mind map, for example sketches of drops of blood on the iron mind map will remind you that iron is needed for healthy red blood cells.

Now test yourself

1 Name four foods that are a good source of protein. (4 marks)
2 State the two main groups of carbohydrates. (2 marks)
3 Describe two functions of water in the body. (2 marks)
4 Describe two functions of vitamin C in the diet. (2 marks)
5 Name three foods that are a good source of calcium. (3 marks)

1.2 Nutritional needs of specific groups

Different life stages

REVISED

Nutritional needs change from birth until old age, so the age range of different groups needs to be taken into consideration when planning a menu to suit them.

Childhood

- Young children go through rapid **growth spurts** as well as usually having a very active lifestyle. This increases the need for more energy (calories) in the diet. ✓
- As children's stomachs are small, they cannot eat large meals at one time. They need to eat regular, smaller meals as well as having snacks and drinks throughout the day to provide sufficient energy and nutrients.
- Children's menus should meet their nutritional needs and appeal to them. ✓
- Children's diets should be varied. ✓
- It is important that children develop good eating habits so they establish these throughout their lives.
- The body goes through many changes when children become teenagers. Teenagers, like younger children, also have rapid growth spurts.
- It is important for teenagers to follow the principles of the **Eatwell Guide** (see page 110) to ensure a good balance of foods and nutrients.

Adulthood

- Adults still need a **well-balanced diet** to ensure they have the correct nutrients in the right quantities.
- The Eatwell Guide should be followed by adults to ensure this balance.

Later adulthood

- Older adults still need a well-balanced diet containing all of the nutrients in the correct proportions. Following the Eatwell Guide is important.
- Fewer calories (energy) are needed in later life as our bodies tend to slow down and we become less active.
- Older adults are less efficient at absorbing nutrients; their diet needs to be planned carefully so that the maximum nutrients may be obtained from smaller amounts of food.
- Sugary and fatty foods should be avoided as these contain a lot of energy which, if eaten too often, may lead to becoming overweight or obese.

> **Nutritional needs:** which nutrients in particular an individual or group needs.
>
> **Growth spurt:** a rapid increase in height.
>
> **Eatwell Guide:** government recommendations on eating healthily and achieving a balanced diet.
>
> **Well-balanced diet:** a diet that contains all the nutrients in the correct amounts to meet individual needs.

Figure 6.2 Children eating out

Figure 6.3 A healthy diet and regular exercise slow down the effects of ageing

LO1 Understand the importance of nutrition when planning menus

Special diets

Some people follow a special diet for **health** reasons, for example they want to improve their health by eating less sugar, salt and fat and by eating more dietary fibre (NSP).

Others choose to avoid certain foods in their diets for **ethical** reasons, for example vegetarians do not eat meat and vegans do not eat any animal products.

- Vegetarians do not eat meat, fish or any food that involves the killing of an animal, for example lard or gelatine. Lacto vegetarians eat **dairy products**; ovo-lacto vegetarians eat eggs and dairy products.

- Vegans are strict vegetarians that do not eat any animal products, including dairy products, eggs and honey. This is becoming more popular in the UK for ethical reasons as well as increasing concerns about the environmental impact of producing animal foods (see page 107).

Some **religions** do not allow people to eat certain foods, for example Jewish people do not eat shellfish or pork, and Hindus do not eat beef.

Medical conditions

Medical conditions can also require a special diet.

Food intolerances describe when people are sensitive to certain foods and may have difficulty digesting them.

> **Health**: being free from illness or injury.
>
> **Ethical**: making choices based on opinions of right and wrong.
>
> **Dairy products**: milk from mammals (usually cows) as well as foods made from milk, such as yoghurt, cheese, cream and butter.

Figure 6.4 **This symbol means the food is suitable for vegetarians**

Table 6.4 **Food intolerances and which foods to avoid**

Food intolerance	Foods that should be avoided
Lactose	Lactose is the sugar in milk, so anything with milk in it should be avoided, for example: ● milk ● yoghurt ● cheese ● cream. Check ingredients labels for 'milk', as it is added to many different foods.
Gluten	Gluten is the protein found in wheat and other cereals, such as rye and barley; the following foods should be avoided unless you are sure they are gluten free: ● pasta ● cakes ● biscuits ● breakfast cereals ● bread ● sauces.
Soy	Soy comes from soybeans (also called edamame beans). Soybean products are widely used in the food industry, especially soya flour, so check food labels. The following foods often contain soy: ● bread ● cakes ● ready meals. Any ready-made product may use soy as a food additive.

Food allergies describe a more serious reaction when eating the food may cause life-threatening symptoms.

In Europe, food allergens are monitored and assessed by experts. They give advice on which foods need to be labelled on prepacked food. Businesses must emphasise these allergens. Businesses that sell loose food must provide written or verbal information about food allergens.

Cereals containing gluten

Peanuts

Nuts

Milk

Soya

Mustard

Lupin

Eggs

Fish

Crustaceans

Molluscs

Sesame seeds

Celery

Sulphur dioxide

Figure 6.5 Ingredients that can cause food allergies or reactions

Activity levels

Your body needs energy for every function and movement it performs, for example:

- breathing
- the function of **internal organs**
- digesting food
- activities such as walking, running, cycling and even sitting down.

Your energy needs change depending on the activities you do, as well as your age, health and gender.

The amount of energy you need to stay alive for 24 hours when warm and resting is known as your **basal metabolic rate (BMR)**.

Your **physical activity level (PAL)** shows your daily activity level as a number. If you are not very active you will have a lower PAL than someone who is very active.

PAL and BMR can be used to work out how much energy is needed from food in order to maintain your lifestyle.

$$\text{Physical activity level} = \frac{\textit{Total energy expenditure over 24 hours}}{\textit{Basal metabolic rate over 24 hours}}$$

Internal organs: organ inside the human body, beneath the skin, for example the stomach, heart, lungs, and liver.

Figure 6.6 Your age, gender and physical activity level affects how much energy you need per day

You will need to compare the nutritional needs of specific groups, for example children and older adults, in your internal assessment. To gain high marks you need to give clear and in-depth reasons for the similarities and differences, for example:

Children are growing and active, therefore they need a well-balanced diet following the Eatwell Guide, which will provide nutrients and energy for growth, repair and maintenance. Older adults require less energy in their diets as their metabolic rate slows down and they become less active, which can cause muscles to weaken. Their bodies become less efficient at absorbing nutrients, so their diet needs to be carefully planned so that the maximum nutrients may be obtained from smaller amounts of food.

Separate your work into paragraphs, making it very clear which specific group you are writing about. Remember to compare the similarities and differences between their nutritional needs.

Draw a mind map for each of the three main life stages – children, adults and older adults – showing the different nutritional needs. Suggest a simple lunch suitable for each group.

When comparing the nutritional needs of two groups some students do not plan how they are going to lay out their work, and the information presented can be difficult to read and understand. The focus moves from one specific group to the other without explanation.

Now test yourself

TESTED ☐

1 Give two reasons why children need smaller, regular meals than adults. (2 marks)
2 Describe a vegan diet and explain why this diet is becoming more popular in the UK. (4 marks)
3 State three foods that are **not** suitable for someone with lactose intolerance. (3 marks)
4 Explain why it is important that food labels emphasise ingredients that could cause an allergic reaction in some pe ople. (3 marks)
5 State what each of the following abbreviations stands for. (2 marks)
   ● PAL
   ● BMR

1.3 Characteristics of unsatisfactory nutritional intake

● The food you eat affects how healthy you are.
● You should follow the principles of the Eatwell Guide, and should not overeat or under-eat, to achieve a healthy, balanced diet.
● **Nutritional deficiency** means eating too little food or too little of a nutrient to meet dietary needs.
● **Nutritional excess** means eating too much food or too much of a nutrient.
● Eating too much or too little of a nutrient can have an impact on your health. These impacts may be visible or invisible.

Nutritional deficiency: eating too little food or too little of a nutrient to meet dietary needs.

Nutritional excess: eating too much food or too much of a nutrient.

Table 6.5 Characteristics of nutritional deficiencies and excesses

Nutrient	Nutritional deficiency (too little)	Nutritional excess (too much)
Protein	Poor growth Thinning hair or hair loss Catch infections easily, for example colds Fluid under their skin (oedema)	Puts strain on kidneys and liver Increased weight, as extra protein is converted into fat
Fats	Weight loss Lack of essential fatty acids Lack of vitamins A, D, E and K	Weight gain Obesity Raises bad **cholesterol** levels in the body Risk of type 2 **diabetes**, **high blood pressure** and **coronary heart disease**
Carbohydrates	Loss of fat and weight Poor growth in children	Increase in body fat and weight, leading to obesity Too much sugar causes tooth decay
Dietary fibre	Constipation Increased risk of bowel cancer	Too much fibre can reduce the body's ability to absorb iron and calcium
Vitamin A	Night blindness	Poisonous if eaten in large amounts Pregnant women should avoid foods high in vitamin A
Vitamins B1, B2 and B3	B1 – **beriberi** B2 – dry and cracked lips B3 – **pellagra**	No harmful side effects
Vitamin B9	Red blood cells do not function properly (a type of **anaemia**) Birth defects in babies, such as spina bifida	No harmful side effects
Vitamin B12	Red blood cells do not function properly (a type of anaemia)	No harmful side effects
Vitamin C	**Scurvy**	Stomach pain Diarrhoea
Vitamin D	**Rickets** in babies and toddlers **Osteoporosis** in adults	Excessive dietary vitamin D intake can have toxic effects and may lead to hypercalcaemia (high calcium levels in the blood)
Vitamin K	Blood doesn't clot properly	No harmful side effects
Calcium	Rickets in babies and toddlers Osteoporosis in adults	Stomach pain Diarrhoea Hypercalcaemia
Iron	Iron-deficiency anaemia	Constipation Feeling sick Stomach pain
Sodium	Essential to balance fluids in the body, such as blood	High blood pressure Strokes Heart attacks
Fluoride	Tooth enamel can become weak, which causes tooth decay	Staining and pits can develop on the teeth
Phosphorus	Unlikely to be deficient in the diet as found in many foods	Bones become weak as excess phosphorus can prevent calcium from being absorbed

Cholesterol: a fatty substance found in the blood; it is essential for humans but too much can be harmful.

Diabetes: a condition where the body's sugar levels cannot be controlled properly.

High blood pressure: a higher than normal force of blood pressing against the arteries.

Coronary heart disease: the heart's blood supply is blocked or interrupted by a build-up of fatty substances in the coronary arteries.

Beriberi: a disease caused by a lack of vitamin B1; it causes inflammation of the nerves and heart failure.

Pellagra: a disease caused by a lack of vitamin B3; it causes inflammation of the skin, diarrhoea, fatigue and memory loss.

Anaemia: a condition that affects the red blood cells in the body; it reduces the amount of oxygen that can be carried in the blood, leading to fatigue and breathlessness.

Scurvy: an illness caused by a lack of vitamin C; it causes swollen, bleeding gums.

Rickets: a condition found in children where a lack of vitamin D and calcium in the diet causes the bones to soften.

Osteoporosis: a condition found in adults where a loss of calcium from bones makes them weak and more likely to break.

Revision activity

Make some flash cards of the key words in this section. On one side write the word and on the other the definition. Practise with a friend until you know them by heart.

Typical mistake

Some students do not gain high marks for this assessment criteria as they describe the main characteristics of an unsatisfactory nutritional intake, but they do not explain a wide enough range of nutrients; for example, they may just include the need for 'vitamins' and 'minerals' without explaining specific micronutrients. To gain high marks you need to give detailed information, for example:

Vitamin C is especially important for teenage girls as it helps them to absorb iron, which is needed for healthy red blood cells. Teenage girls have a high requirement for the mineral iron due to menstruation. A lack of iron can cause anaemia.

Assessment tip

You need to be able to explain the characteristics of unsatisfactory nutritional intake, which groups of people may be affected and how in your internal assessment. The highest mark that can be awarded for this assessment criteria is a Level 2 merit. To achieve this, you will need to explain with clear reasoning the characteristics of unsatisfactory intake of a range of nutrients. Your explanations should be related to specific groups of people, for example children or adults.

Now test yourself

TESTED ☐

1 Describe the difference between nutritional deficiency and nutritional excess. (2 marks)
2 Explain why it is important to have some fat in your diet. (3 marks)
3 Describe what happens to your body if you do not have enough fibre in your diet. (2 marks)
4 State the names of two diseases caused by a lack of vitamin D in the diet. (2 marks)
5 Explain the effects of having a nutritional deficiency and a nutritional excess of iron in the diet. (4 marks)

1.4 How cooking methods impact on nutritional value

Different cooking methods can have an impact on the nutritional value of food.

Table 6.6 lists different cooking methods and describes how they can change the nutrients in food. For healthy eating we should select cooking methods that retain as many vitamins and minerals as possible, and take care not to increase the fat content of food very much.

> **Leach**: to dissolve or drain off into a liquid.
>
> **Water-soluble vitamins**: vitamins that dissolve in water, for example the B group vitamins and vitamin C.
>
> **Fat-soluble vitamins**: vitamins that dissolve in fat, for example vitamins A, D, E and K.

Table 6.6 Impact on the nutritional value of food of different cooking methods

Cooking method	Impact on the nutritional value of food
Boiling	Vitamin C and some B group vitamins are destroyed by heat Vitamin C, B group vitamins, iron and calcium **leach** into the cooking water No added fat
Steaming	No contact with water, so vitamin C, B group vitamins, iron and calcium will not leach out Some **water-soluble vitamins** ... e effect of the heat (B group vitamins and v... No ad...
Baking	Does... Vitam... Some ... etary fibre (for example, potatoes and bu... No add...
Grilling	Most v... , but some are lost due to the intense... Fat is r... Iron an... **Fat-solu**... because they will run out of the food No adde...
Stir-frying	Quick m...... so most vitamin C and B group vitamins are retained Small amount of oil means that it is a healthier cooking method than other types of frying Fat-soluble vitamins are added
Roasting	Does not affect calcium and iron Vitamin C and B group vitamins are lost due to the heat and long cooking time Adds fat to food, including fat-soluble vitamins
Poaching	Some vitamin C, B group vitamins, iron and calcium will leach into the cooking water The heat will destroy some of the vitamin C and B group vitamins No added fat

(handwritten note: make some links to students too. Students – too much sugar – lead to...)

Revision activity

Make some flash cards to show the different cookery methods and how the nutrients are affected during each cooking method. With a partner, test each other on each method until you have both learnt them.

Typical mistake

Some students fail to identify all the cooking methods in their chosen dishes and so don't gain the highest marks. The evidence they give is vague and often refers generally to losing vitamins rather than naming the vitamins groups (for example, fat-soluble vitamins) or specific vitamins (for example, B group vitamins).

Assessment tip

To get a high mark in your internal assessment you need to explain how cooking methods impact on nutritional value. The highest mark you can achieve for this assessment criterion is a Level 2 pass. To gain this top mark, you will need to explain how this happens and give the specific names of vitamins and minerals affected.

Now test yourself

TESTED

1 Explain why it is important to choose cooking methods that retain the nutrients in food. (3 marks)
2 Describe the nutritional changes when grilling meat sausages. (2 marks)
3 Compare boiling and steaming, and explain which method you would you recommend for cooking broccoli. (4 marks)
4 Select two methods of cooking you would describe as quick and healthy. Explain your answer. (4 marks)
5 Describe the nutritional changes for baking compared to roasting when cooking potatoes. (4 marks)

Answers and quick quizzes at **www.hoddereducation.co.uk/myrevisionnotes**

Unit 2 LO2 Understand menu planning

2.1 Factors to consider when proposing dishes for menus

Time of year

REVISED

- Some foods are seasonal, which means they are only available at certain times of the year.
- Many fruits and vegetables grown in the UK are seasonal.
- Developments in transport, and the **preservation** and storage of foods, means that we can import foods from other countries that are not in season in the UK, as well as foods that we cannot grow. This means that much of our food is available all year round.
- Some events are planned to match the season, for example outdoor events such as barbecues or picnics may be held in the summer. In the winter, at Christmas time, meal planning may be focused on a traditional Christmas dinner, including roast turkey with roast potatoes and vegetables.
- The time of year affects the type of food that is on the menu, for example eating hot food such as soup and curries on a cold day, or cool salads and ice cream on a hot day.

> **Preservation**: treatment of food to prevent decay and to keep it safe for longer periods of time.

Figure 7.1 Strawberries are an example of a seasonal food

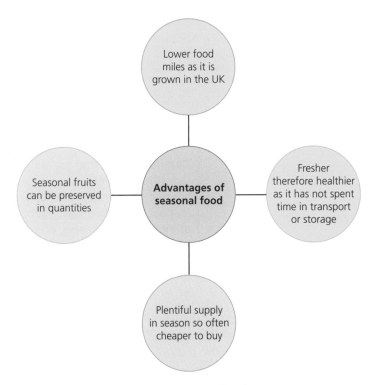

Figure 7.2 **Advantages of seasonal foods**

Skills of staff

- Staff will need excellent cookery skills, food safety knowledge, leadership and management skills, **budgeting skills**, the ability to work under pressure (often in a limited space) to meet deadlines, and the ability to keep calm in stressful situations.
- Chefs need precise practical skills, such as the weighing and measuring of ingredients for recipes that require accurate and consistent amounts.
- Different types of chefs specialise in different areas of food preparation and cooking, for example pastry chefs make bread, pastries, cakes, **confectionery**, decorated cakes, batters, desserts and other baked goods. They may be in charge of the dessert menu.

> **Budgeting skills**: skills of managing money by prioritising essential spending before optional spending.
>
> **Confectionery**: sweets and chocolate.

Equipment available

A range of food preparation and cooking equipment may be needed to create certain dishes. There are three main types of equipment:

- **Hand-held equipment**, such as knives, tins and pans. These come in different sizes and shapes for different uses and help to produce quality foods.
- **Powered equipment**, such as blenders, processors, mixing machines, deep-fat fryers and cookers. Powered equipment can save time; for example, food processors can grate, mix, blend and chop in a very quick time compared to carrying out these tasks by hand.
- **Food storage equipment**, such as blast chillers, fridges and freezers. A blast chiller can chill cooked food ready for **decorating**, for example choux pastry. Freezers can prolong the shelf life of many different foods and help to avoid food waste (see page 148).

Figure 7.3 A deep-fat fryer is a piece of specialist equipment

It would be very difficult to make some dishes without specialist equipment. For example, a blender is very useful when making smooth soup; without a blender the soup would have to be pushed through a sieve, which is very time-consuming.

> **Decorating**: finishing off dishes before serving, for example piping cream on gateaux.

Time available

- If there is a short amount of time available to cook, serve and eat the food, then the range of food offered on the menu will need to be limited. Fast-food outlets have a smaller menu of pre-prepared components so they can cook and serve the food quickly.
- It is essential that time is managed appropriately by the chef and their team to ensure the waiting time for customers is acceptable, and that the time waiting between courses is appropriate for the venue.
- To assist with time management, many **components of dishes** can be prepared in advance, for example the chopping of vegetables. Some dishes can be made in advance and to be reheated or baked, for example soups, cottage pie and lasagne. Many cold desserts can be pre-made so they will be ready to serve.

> **Components of dishes**: ingredients already combined together; they can be purchased this way, such as ready-made pastry, or partly prepared by the chef, for example washed and drained salad ready for use.

Type of provision

The type of food provision will affect the dishes that are served.

Table 7.1 Typical food provision of different catering options

Food service	Description
Formal restaurant	Food is usually served to customers by waiting staff. Meals are served, for example a three-course meal – starter, main and dessert
Street food	Ready-to-eat food or drink sold on the street or in a public place, such as at a market or festival. Food provision may be a main dish or dessert. Food is served with disposable plates/cutlery
Self-service	Customers help themselves to food, for example a carvery
Fast food	Food is made to order very quickly and can be taken away from the restaurant or stall to eat; seats and tables are often provided
Cafeteria	Small or inexpensive restaurant or coffee bar. Main meals and lighter meals are available, as well as snacks and hot/cold drinks
Takeaway	Takeaway restaurants (for example Chinese, Indian and pizzas) take an order and deliver the food to the customer's home; customers can also order at the restaurant and then take the food away to eat it
Buffet	A selection of dishes is laid out for customers to help themselves; different buffet styles include: ● sit-down buffet – often a main meal and desserts with lots of choices; usually eaten with a knife and fork at a table ● stand-up or fork buffet – lighter meals are served, often savoury and sweet; mainly cold food ● finger buffet – light savoury and sweet food in small portion sizes, ready to eat with fingers or from a cocktail stick
Plate	The meal ordered is plated up and brought to the customer's table by a waiter. This can be in a formal restaurant or a cafe
Waiting service	The food is served to customers at the table by waiting staff. This service is provided in restaurants, some cafes and B&Bs
Automatic vending	Drinks and snacks are stored in a machine with a glass front and items are selected by the customer; they are often coin/card operated and placed in establishments where it may not always be possible to get access to food, for example colleges and hospitals
Hotel	Provides overnight accommodation and food and drink options Many hotels offer breakfast, evening meals, bar snacks, lunch and room service (food ordered and delivered to your room); budget hotels usually have a simpler offering
Bed and breakfast	Offers overnight accommodation and breakfast; often these are private family homes where rooms are made available to guests; breakfast is usually served plated up in a dining room or the owner's kitchen

Finance

● Food costs form a large percentage of the total costs of a catering establishment. It is therefore essential that dishes are costed accurately.

● Food costs need to be controlled so that the catering establishment makes a profit and stays in business.

● When buying food, it is important to order the correct amount of the best quality food at the best price.

● It is also important to monitor stock to make sure it is rotated, so that the oldest food is used up first, which reduces waste.

L02 Understand menu planning

- Recipes should be followed so that the exact amount of ingredients needed are bought and used. Weighing and measuring are crucial too.
- It is important to know how much a recipe is going to cost to make when preparing and cooking food.
- The pricing of menu items should be what customers expect and are willing to pay for each dish/meal.

Client base

- The client base will depend on the area and the type of catering establishment – its standards, its size and who the venue is targeting.
- Customers need dishes and meals that are varied and include a range of colours, flavours, textures and temperatures.
- You need to consider your client base and make menu choices that are suitable for the needs of your clients.
- There should be options for special diets, for example gluten-free and vegetarian diets.
- Some dishes should be suitable for people following certain religions, for example kosher or halal food for customers that are Jewish or Muslim.

Revision activity

Copy and complete the table to give examples of different types of kitchen equipment. An example for each has been completed for you.

Hand-held equipment	Powered equipment	Food storage equipment
Knives	Blenders	Fridges

For each piece of equipment, give an example of a dish it could be used to produce.

Assessment tip

This unit is about planning menus carefully. To get a high mark in your internal assessment you need to be able to explain factors to consider when proposing dishes for menus.

The highest mark available for this assessment criterion is a Level 2 merit. To achieve this you will need to clearly explain customer needs, business needs, and what is needed for the preparation and cooking of the selected menu items. The choices and explanations should all be relevant and well justified.

Typical mistake

Students often make the mistake of choosing foods they like themselves for their menu, rather than those that are suitable for the customers, venue and occasion in the question. The foods should be suitable for the specific group(s) you are catering for (for example vegetarians, young children or religious groups). Not providing clear reasons for your choices will mean you lose marks.

Now test yourself

1 State two advantages of putting seasonal foods on a menu.   (2 marks)
2 Describe two essential skills a successful chef should have.   (2 marks)
3 List three advantages of having a wide range of kitchen equipment. Give examples in
   your answer.   (6 marks)
4 Copy and complete the following table to match these specific groups – younger adults,
   teenagers, older adults – to a type of food service and explain your choices.   (6 marks)

Type of food service	Specific group	Why?
Restaurant – waiting staff service		
Fast food – counter service		
Carvery – self-service		

5 Explain why it is important that all menu items are costed and the selling price calculated
   before putting a menu together.   (2 marks)

2.2 How dishes on a menu address environmental issues

Food production has a huge impact on the environment. Some types of food production have more of an effect than others. For example, rearing animals for food produces far more **greenhouse gases** than plant-based protein food, such as beans.

A **carbon footprint** is a measurement of the amount of carbon dioxide released into the atmosphere from industry, transport, groups of people and individuals. The carbon footprint of food can be measured by recording the carbon dioxide and other greenhouse gases that are released from the farm where the food is grown, reared or caught right through to the place where the food is consumed.

- Animal foods, such as meat, dairy products and eggs, have a high carbon footprint; this is bad for the environment.
- Plant foods, such as vegetables, fruits, nuts, beans and cereals, have a lower carbon footprint; this is better for the environment.

> **Greenhouse gases**: gases that trap heat and raise the Earth's temperature, for example carbon dioxide, methane and nitrous oxide.
>
> **Carbon footprint**: a measure of the impact humans have on the environment in terms of the amount of greenhouse gases produced by a particular product or industry.

Dishes

Preparation and cooking methods

A lot of energy is used in the preparation and cooking of food. We need to reduce this to protect our environment.

To save energy during preparation you could use **mechanical equipment** instead of electrical equipment, for example chop, cut, slice, grate, shred and whisk using hand skills.

To save energy during cooking you should:

- fill the oven up when cooking, so the whole meal is cooked together
- use a tiered steamer for cooking vegetables, so only one hob is needed
- use a microwave oven to cook food quickly

> **Mechanical equipment**: equipment powered by humans.

- use lids on saucepans, match the size of the pan to the size of the ring and, when using gas, the flames should remain under the pan for maximum efficiency
- use quick methods of cooking, such as stir-frying.

Ingredients used

- **Sustainable ingredients**: choose foods that have been farmed in a way that maintains and improves the environment.
- **Seasonal ingredients**: these are available only at certain times in the year. English strawberries, for example, are at their best in June and July.
- **Organic foods**: foods produced without the use of **artificial fertilisers**; **pesticides** are restricted; there are high welfare standards for animals, which are always free range; the use of drugs and antibiotics is restricted; there are high standards of environmental protection.
- **Locally sourced**: this often means that the food is produced within 30 miles of the place where it is purchased; it means there will be a lower carbon footprint.
- **Farm assured**: the farms and food companies meet high standards of food safety and hygiene, animal welfare and environmental protection.

Packaging

- Food packaging can cause environmental problems as it uses up natural resources such as oil, metals and trees.
- Packaging can cause pollution; some may not be suitable for recycling so ends up being incinerated or buried in **landfill sites**.

Figure 7.4 The Red Tractor logo shows the food product is traceable, safe and responsibly produced

---

Artificial fertilisers: man-made chemicals that increase the yield of crops.

Pesticides: chemicals used to destroy insects or other organisms that could harm crops.

Landfill site: a site where rubbish is buried in the ground.

Environmental issues

REVISED

Conservation of energy and water

The environment includes the air, water and land on which people, animals and plants live. To protect our environment, we need to:

- use less energy
- avoid waste
- reduce our consumption of water
- recycle and reuse as much as possible.

Reduce, reuse, recycle

Table 7.2 Practical ways to reduce, reuse and recycle

Reduce	Cut down on the amount of packaging on food
	Conserve energy and water when cooking
	Reduce the use of processed foods, which require a lot of energy to manufacture them
	By using more plant foods rather than animal foods, we can hugely reduce water consumption (animals require large amounts of water throughout their lives before slaughter)
Reuse	Reuse packaging, such as jars and plastic containers, rather than throwing them away
	Use leftover food to create another dish, for example: • use leftover cake to make a trifle • use leftover meat in a shepherd's pie • use leftover chicken in a curry • use leftover potato in fish cakes or a frittata
Recycle	Clean and dry food packaging can usually be recycled, for example glass, metal, card, paper and some plastics

Sustainability

- A sustainable environment is one where the demands placed on it can be met without reducing its ability to allow all people to live well, now and in the future.

- **Food miles** are the distance food has to travel from where it is grown, reared or caught to reach the consumer. The lower the food miles, the more sustainable the food product is. Therefore, buying locally produced food and growing your own fruit and vegetables is better for the environment.

- **Food provenance** means knowing where our food has come from and knowing how ingredients are grown, reared or caught and then transported to us.

> **Food miles**: the distance food has to travel from where it is grown, reared or caught to reach the consumer.
>
> **Food provenance**: knowing where our food has come from and knowing how ingredients are grown, reared and caught and then transported to us.

Revision activity

Use a leftover ingredient to design a dish suitable for two teenagers. If possible, the rest of the ingredients should be environmentally friendly, for example unprocessed and locally produced.

List the ingredients in a table to show how they have less impact on the environment. An example has been completed for you below:

Name of ingredient	Benefits to the environment
Leftover cold chicken	Saves the food from being wasted and possibly going to landfill
Wholewheat pasta	Less processed than white pasta, so less energy is needed to produce it
Homegrown peas	Grown at home, so zero food miles
Local tomatoes – organic	Grown locally, so less food miles They are organic so they are grown without artificial fertilisers and pesticides

Assessment tip

To get a high mark in your internal assessment you need to explain how dishes on a menu address environmental issues. The top grade for this assessment criterion is a Level 2 pass. You need to explain how environmental issues can be addressed with lots of detail.

Typical mistake

As there are not so many marks for this criterion, some students rush this part and just outline environmental issues in a very general way. To gain higher marks, itemise the ingredients and discuss each one separately if relevant.

Now test yourself

TESTED

1. Name three greenhouse gases. (3 marks)
2. Describe what is meant by the term 'carbon footprint'. (2 marks)
3. Explain why plant foods are less damaging on the environment than animal foods. (2 marks)
4. State four different choices you could make when choosing, preparing and cooking ingredients for a meal that would benefit the environment. (4 marks)
5. You have some leftover mashed potato. Name three different dishes you could make with this potato. (3 marks)

2.3 How menu dishes meet customer needs

Customers will have varying needs when eating from a menu. It is important for staff to know what these specific needs are when catering for every customer. This may include special diets, such as vegetarian and vegan, allergies and intolerances, or avoiding foods for religious reasons.

Nutritional

● The nutritional needs of a customer should be considered carefully when planning a menu (see page 95 for the nutritional needs of specific groups).

● Eating out is a regular occurrence for many families rather than just for special occasions, so healthy eating is a priority. The Eatwell Guide shows the government recommendations for a healthy and balanced diet. It is recommended for all ages from two years of age.

● Nutritional needs change from birth until old age, so the age range of customers should be taken into consideration when planning a menu to suit them.

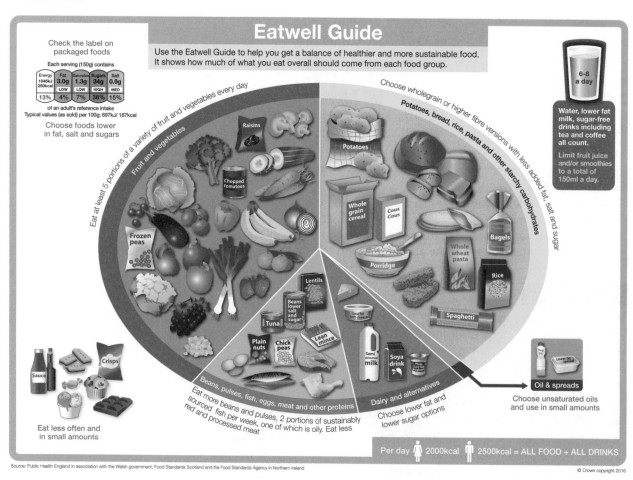

Figure 7.5 The Eatwell Guide shows how different foods can contribute to a healthy, balanced diet

Answers and quick quizzes at www.hoddereducation.co.uk/myrevisionnotes

Organoleptic

- When we eat food, we use our five senses: sight, smell, touch, taste and sound.
- The word **organoleptic** means the qualities of food that people experience with their senses. This is also known as sensory analysis or sensory evaluation.
- Eating food should be an enjoyable experience. When planning a menu, dishes that most people find **appetising** and that appeal to their senses should be selected.

> **Organoleptic**: using the senses to assess the qualities of food.
>
> **Appetising**: food that appeals to your senses.

Figure 7.6 When planning dishes, select food that appeals to the senses

Cost

- Cost needs to be considered when planning menus (see page 105).
- Different food services offer food at a wide range of prices to meet the needs of different customers.
- If a new restaurant is moving into an area, the managers would need to check out the competition and see what is already available and the range of prices that are being charged. There may be a **gap in the market** for a restaurant with a different price range, for example high-priced fine dining option in an area that currently offers only low- to mid-price ranged menus.
- Most customers like to have good value for money and to know that they are getting a good deal. Restaurants may offer incentives for customers to visit again, for example student discounts, theme nights (such as an Italian evening) or vouchers for money off a future meal if they return in a specified time.

> **Gap in the market**: an unmet consumer demand.

Revision activity

Using a menu from a restaurant, identify the nutritional needs that have been met as well as any healthy eating information. Choose a meal from the menu – a main course and a dessert – and describe the organoleptic qualities of each food in your chosen dishes.

Typical mistake

Some students consider the organoleptic qualities and cost of meals carefully, but don't consider good nutrition. A well-balanced meal is needed that follows the healthy eating guidelines of the Eatwell Guide. If you do not provide reasons for your explanations, you will not reach the highest marks.

Now test yourself

TESTED

1 Name two types of special diets and which foods should be avoided in each diet. (2 marks)
2 List the six food groups from the Eatwell Guide in descending order by size (biggest first). (6 marks)
3 Describe the organoleptic qualities of:
   a) tomato soup (2 marks)
   b) crudités (raw celery, cucumber and carrot sticks) (2 marks)
   c) chocolate ice cream (2 marks)
4 Explain why restaurants need to cost their recipes carefully before deciding how much to charge for menu items. (2 marks)
5 Explain why it is important for restaurants and cafes to have menu items with a range of prices. (3 marks)

Assessment tip

To get a high mark in your internal assessment you need to explain how the dishes you have chosen for your menu meet the needs of specified customers. This assessment criterion covers the nutritional value, organoleptic qualities and the cost of food. You will need to make sure your explanations are comprehensive and well reasoned.

2.4 Planning production of dishes for a menu

The dishes on a menu are the starting point for planning how and when they will be produced. This requires careful organisation. After the menu items have been chosen, the order of work and the times when everything should happen should be planned so that the food is prepared, cooked and served on time, while ensuring it is presented well and is safe to eat.

Sequencing

REVISED

The order in which the different dishes on a menu are produced is known as **sequencing**. It is also known as **dovetailing**.

Correct sequencing will ensure that the quality of the dishes matches what is expected by the customers. It will include:

● the times when tasks need to be started and finished
● the staff needed for different tasks
● the equipment needed at each stage
● which dishes need to be prepared first – some foods, such as chicken or tofu, may be marinated the night before while others, such as stir-fry vegetables, may be prepared early on in the day but not fried until just before serving so that they retain their texture, flavour and colour.

Sequencing: preparing and cooking dishes in a suitable order so that the dishes are ready to serve on time.

Dovetailing: preparing part of one dish and then part of another dish before the first dish is finished.

Timing

REVISED

Good timing is very important when preparing meals for customers, so that the food is cooked properly and the meal is prepared and served in a reasonable time. In addition, each course should be served together at each table.

The time taken for preparation tasks – such as peeling carrots, scrubbing potatoes, filleting fish, freezing ice cream or cooling pastry before filling and decorating – should be known or carefully estimated.

These timings will allow planning for each stage of the recipe and help to organise which staff and equipment are needed at each stage of preparation, cooking and serving.

Table 7.3 shows the timings that should be considered as part of your production plan.

Table 7.3 Key terms for a production plan

Mise en place	*Mise en place* means preparation before cooking starts, for example: ● organising equipment and ingredients before you start preparing and cooking food ● reading and understanding each stage of the recipe ● preparing food carefully to avoid wastage
Cooking	Cooking food correctly is essential to make sure the food is of a high quality, safe to eat and enjoyed by its customers
Cooling	Making sure that hot food is cooled to below 8 °C within 90 minutes to prevent bacteria from multiplying
Hot holding	Keeping hot food at a temperature of 63 °C for a maximum of two hours to ensure its quality and safety before serving to customers
Completion	Finishing off dishes by **garnishing**, decorating and making the food look appetising, as well as checking the temperatures are correct to serve to customers Make sure you factor time for completion into your production plan
Serving	Orders should be completed and served together so that everyone at the table can eat at the same time Food should be served hygienically, for example by using tongs rather than bare hands
Waste	Food wastage should be reduced as much as possible by careful stock control, providing correct portion sizes for different customers and preparing food skilfully, for example peeling vegetables thinly to avoid wasting too much food
Equipment	Many different types of equipment are used in a catering kitchen; you need to think about all of the equipment you need to produce your dishes, including: ● large equipment, for example ovens and blast chillers ● small equipment, for example knives, mixing bowls and chopping boards ● mechanical equipment, for example food mixers and ice cream machines ● safety equipment, for example first aid kit and fire extinguishers
Commodity quantities	These need to be ordered in advance, so the correct amount of ingredients for each recipe needs be carefully estimated to provide the correct portion size for customers
Tools	Tools is the name given to the wide range of equipment found in a kitchen: it can be divided into groups: ● utensils: includes small items, such as a sieve or grater, as well as large, such as a pasta machine or a manual ice cream maker ● cooking utensils: for example frying pans, ramekin dishes and cake tins ● kitchen equipment ● plating-up utensils: ladles, sauce bottles for coulis ● table setting: knives, forks and spoons, salad servers, pizza wheels, salt and pepper grinders Make sure you plan all of the tools you need for your dishes
Contingencies	A contingency is a back-up plan that you can put into place if things go wrong, for example having some spare ingredients in case a recipe goes wrong and you need to start again with new ingredients Consider contingencies as part of your production planning
Health, safety and hygiene	Staff need to trained to store food correctly and to use equipment in a safe and hygienic way, to ensure that the food served is safe to eat Staff training is needed so that they can give information on allergens to customers Consider the health, safety and hygiene aspects of all stages in the preparation, cooking and serving of your dishes
Quality points	Each commodity will have quality points that should be checked before using in recipes, for example fresh fish should smell fresh (like the sea), and their eyes should be clear and bright and not sunken in
Storage	Storage is needed for ingredients as well as for the equipment, tools and materials used in a catering kitchen Food temperatures need to be checked to make sure they are correct (see page 147). All equipment and food should be stored tidily and hygienically, ready for use

When you have considered all of these points, you will be ready to make your production plan. You will need:

- a list of ingredients and method for each recipe
- all the equipment for each stage of the recipe
- step-by-step instructions for the preparation, making and presentation of dishes
- correct timings.

> *Mise en place*: preparation before starting to cook.
>
> **Garnishes**: decorations on savoury food dishes.

Table 7.4 A sample production plan for Bolognese sauce (green) and cheesecake (red)

Time	Activity	Special points
Step 1 10 minutes 9.00–9.10	*Mise-en-place* Wash hands, put apron on, clean table with antibacterial spray Collect **equipment and tools** for making cheesecake and Bolognese sauce Weigh and measure ingredients Wash vegetables	Use antibacterial handwash and spray for the table to ensure that all bacteria are killed Keep high-risk foods, such as cream and meat, separate in the fridge until needed Ensure correct **quantities of commodities** are used **Contingency**: have extra commodities in case of recipe failure
Step 2 10 minutes 9.10–9.20	Crush biscuits, melt margarine in a saucepan, add crushed biscuits Place in cheesecake dish, press crumbs down firmly and chill Slice strawberries	Make sure the pan handle is turned to the side to avoid an accident if the pan is knocked
Step 3 10 minutes 9.20–9.30	Make the cheesecake filling by whisking together the cream cheese, icing sugar and double cream Place a little of the filling in a piping bag Spread the filling on the biscuit base and chill it again	Cream cheese and cream are high-risk foods – take out of the fridge and use them immediately **Storage**: store the cheesecake in the fridge once it has been made Scrape all of the mixture out of the bowl to prevent **food waste**
Step 4 15 minutes 9.30–9.45	Wash up, dry up and put all the equipment away	Use very hot water and washing-up liquid to ensure all the equipment is clean
Step 5 10 minutes 9.45–9.55	Chop all the vegetables for the Bolognese sauce	Use a brown chopping board, and remember to always cut down towards the chopping board
Step 6 10 minutes 9.55–10.05	Place minced beef in a large frying pan Cook until the meat is browned then add the chopped vegetables, tin of tomatoes, 50 ml water, herbs and tomato purée Bring to the boil and then turn down to simmer for 20 minutes on a low heat	Make sure the pan handle is turned to the side to avoid an accident if the pan is knocked Put a lid on the saucepan, unless the sauce is too runny Check sauce is boiling to ensure bacteria are destroyed
Step 7 15 minutes 10.05–10.20	Wash up, dry up and put all the equipment away Stir the meat sauce regularly	Check area is clean and everything stored in the correct place

Table 7.4 A sample production plan for Bolognese sauce (green) and cheesecake (red) (continued)

Time	Activity	Special points
Step 8 10 minutes 10.20–10.30	Take cheesecake out of the fridge, decorate with piped filling and sliced strawberries Return to fridge until ready for marking	**Completion**: quality check the cheesecake – is the piping consistent, are the strawberries cut evenly?
Step 9 15 minutes 10.30–10.45	After 20 mins of simmering, check flavour and then place Bolognese sauce in container Wash up the frying pan Make sure all work surfaces and sinks are wiped down and clean	**Completion**: quality check the sauce – taste using a clean teaspoon and add herbs and seasoning as required **Contingency**: have a selection of serving dishes and choose the best one to match the size and colours of dishes once the recipes are made
Step 10 10 minutes 10.45–10.55	Garnish the sauce, and display the Bolognese sauce and cheesecake together	**Storage**: refrigerate the cheesecake and sauce when cooled down to room temperature

Revision activity

Choose two dishes that you can make in your next practical lesson. Photocopy them and cut out the various stages of each recipe to sequence (dovetail) the methods. Once you are happy with the order, estimate timings for each stage of the recipes. Finally, check all of the key terms are included with sufficient detail in your production plan.

Assessment tip

To get a high mark in your internal assessment you must write up a production plan for your chosen menu dishes. This should include all the timings and dovetailing of activities to make sure all the food is ready to serve at the end of the production plan. Make sure you add contingencies in case things go wrong.

Typical mistakes

Some students write the production plan and put the times on as they go along – this makes it harder and students often run out of time as too long is allowed for each stage. It is easier to write out all of the activities and annotations first and then share the time out evenly to make sure you finish on time.

Now test yourself

TESTED ☐

1 Explain why correct sequencing of the production of dishes is so important. (2 marks)
2 State three important pieces of information that need to be on a production plan. (3 marks)
3 Name three dishes that would need to be prepared at the start of the production plan and explain why this time is needed. (3 marks)
4 Name three dishes that need to be cooked just before serving and explain why. (3 marks)
5 Describe what a contingency plan is. Give four examples of what may be included in a contingency plan when making a traditional Christmas meal for 12 people. (6 marks)

Unit 2 LO3 Be able to cook dishes

3.1 Techniques in preparation of commodities

It is important to know how to prepare a range of food commodities before they are cooked and served.

Techniques

REVISED

Weighing and measuring

Most recipes depend on accurate measurements for success, so it is important to be able to weigh and measure accurately. If you added too much sugar or too much flour when making a cake, for instance, the results are likely to be poor. However, some recipes are more flexible, for example it would not matter if you put two onions in instead of one in a Bolognese sauce.

The following equipment is useful for weighing and measuring:

- **Kitchen scales**: digital/electronic kitchen scales are most widely used.
- **Measuring jug**: a measuring jug is used to measure liquids; the side of the jug is usually marked with millilitres (ml) or fluid ounces (fl oz), or both.
- **Measuring cups**: some American recipes use a cup measurement for dried ingredients such as flour and sugar. Cups should not be used to weigh fat.
- **Measuring spoons**: these are very useful for measuring an accurate teaspoon or tablespoon – one teaspoon is 5 ml, one tablespoon is 15 ml.

Figure 8.1 Digital scales give a more precise and accurate check on weight

Figure 8.2 A measuring jug

Figure 8.3 Measuring spoons

Chopping and slicing

Chopping is to cut food into small pieces of roughly the same size.

Slicing is to cut a thin, broad piece from a large piece of food, for example a slice of cheese or bread. It can also mean to cut a wedge-shaped piece of food from a larger circular piece, for example a slice of pizza, cake or pie.

There are two techniques for chopping and slicing: bridge hold and claw grip.

Bridge hold

1 Use your thumb and forefinger and grip either side of the ingredient.

2 Use the knife to slice the ingredient in the bridge-like gap created by your finger and thumb.

Claw grip

1 With the tips of your fingers and thumb tucked under towards the palm of your hand, hold the ingredient to be cut in a claw-like grip.

2 Hold the knife in your other hand and carefully bring the knife across and slice the ingredient.

> **Chopping**: to cut food into small pieces of roughly the same size.
>
> **Slicing**: to cut a thin, broad piece from a large piece of food, or a wedge-shaped piece from a larger circular piece of food.
>
> **Decorations**: decorations on sweet foods are simply called decorations.

Figure 8.4 **Bridge hold**   Figure 8.5 **Claw grip**

Table 8.1 **Other techniques used to prepare food**

Technique	Description
Shaping	Modelling food to give it an attractive and interesting appearance. Shaping can either be done by hand or by using a piece of equipment. Examples of shaping are: ● making burgers/koftas/meatballs ● making sugarcraft **decorations** ● biscuits using a cutter ● choux pastry using a piping bag.
Peeling	Removing a small amount of the outside skin from fruit and vegetables such as potatoes, carrots, parsnips and apples. A peeler is usually used in this process.
Whisking	When a food is beaten vigorously to trap air into it. A number of pieces of equipment can be used to whisk: ● fork ● balloon whisk ● electric hand-held mixer ● freestanding mixer. Eggs and cream are commonly whisked as both ingredients trap air.

Table 8.1 Other techniques used to prepare food (continued)

Technique	Description
Melting	Using heat to change a solid ingredient into a liquid. Some cakes are made by the melting method, where ingredients such as butter, syrup, sugar or treacle are placed in a saucepan on a low heat until they melt. Chocolate is melted to make decorations or to add it to recipes such as brownies.
Rubbing in	Using fingertips or a food processor to rub fat into flour. This traps air in the mixture, and the flour is coated with a waterproof layer of fat. This prevents the gluten from developing too much to ensure a light, crumbly texture. The rubbing in method is used to make rock cakes, scones, crumbles and pastry.
Sieving	Push ingredients through a sieve to either: ● add air ● remove lumps ● make a smooth sauce, such as a coulis, by removing seeds.
Segmenting	Peeling and dividing into pieces, for example an orange or a grapefruit.
Hydrating	Adding water to an ingredient. Dried mushrooms, couscous and noodles are examples of foods that need hydrating before they are used.
Blending	Mixing two or more ingredients together. This can be done by hand, using a blender (liquidiser) or a food processor. Fruit and yoghurt can be blended together to make smoothies.

Commodities

REVISED

Poultry

● **Poultry** is the name given to birds that are reared for their meat and/or eggs, or both.
● Examples of poultry are chicken, duck, goose and turkey.
● Raw poultry should be prepared on a red chopping board and should be kept well away from cooked foods to avoid **cross-contamination**.

> **Poultry:** the name given to birds that are reared for their meat and/or eggs, or both, such as chicken, duck, goose and turkey.

Answers and quick quizzes at **www.hoddereducation.co.uk/myrevisionnotes**

Preparation techniques for preparing poultry include:

- jointing – poultry can be cut into portions
- filleting – breasts are removed from the chicken
- boning – for example, the bone can be removed from a chicken thigh; a turkey and chicken can be boned and rolled.
- stuffing – stuffing enhances the flavour and texture; the neck-end of the chicken can be stuffed with a flavoured stuffing such as sage and onion or chestnut and cranberry before the chicken is roasted
- flattening – a meat hammer can be used to flatten pieces of chicken; this tenderises it or flattens it ready to be rolled or stuffed
- marinating – poultry can be soaked in a marinade to develop flavour, tenderise it and add colour before cooking.

> **Cross-contamination**: bacteria spreading from another place to another, for example from hands, work surfaces and utensils to food, or from raw meat to cooked meat.

1 Remove the winglets

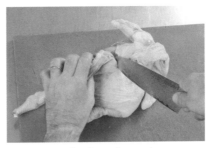
2 Remove the legs from the carcass, cutting around the oyster

3 Cut off the feet

4 Separate the thigh from the drumstick

5 Trim the drumstick neatly

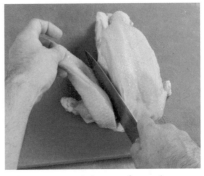
6 Remove each breast from the carcass

7 Separate the wing from the breast and trim it

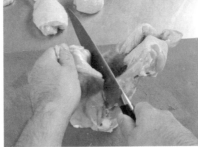
8 Cut into the cavity, splitting the carcass (this may be used for stock)

9 Cut each breast in half

10 The cuts are thighs, wings, breast pieces, drumsticks and winglets

Figure 8.6 Jointing a chicken

Meat

Meat comes mainly from cattle, sheep, pigs, poultry and game.

Table 8.2 Different cuts of meat and meat products

Type of meat	Cuts of meat
Beef	Silverside, shin, steak, topside, brisket
Pork	Leg, chop, shoulder, belly
Bacon and gammon	Cured flesh of a pig
Lamb	Chops, shoulder, leg, shank, breast
Game	Feathered, for example grouse, pheasant, partridge and ostrich
	Furred, for example rabbit, hare and venison
Meat products	Sausages, pies, burgers, pâté

Raw meat should be prepared on a red chopping board, and should be kept well away from cooked foods to avoid cross-contamination.

Preparation techniques for meat include:

- boning – for example, the bone can be removed from a leg of lamb
- flattening – a meat hammer can be used to flatten a piece of meat; this tenderises it or flattens it ready to be rolled or stuffed
- marinating – the meat is soaked in a marinade to develop flavour, tenderise it and add colour before cooking
- trimming – to remove the visible fat from around the meat
- derinding – removing the skin from the outside of bacon and gammon.

Fish

- Fish are classified into three groups: white, oily and shellfish.
- Examples of white fish include cod, haddock, halibut, monkfish, plaice and sea bass.
- Examples of oily fish include herring, kippers, mackerel, salmon, sardines, trout, tuna and whitebait.
- Examples of shellfish include cockles, mussels, oysters, scallops, lobster, prawns and crab.
- Fresh fish is usually sold whole or cut into steaks or fillets.
- Fish sometimes carries food poisoning bacteria, so it is important to follow the same hygienic procedures as when using raw meat.
- A blue chopping board should be used for raw fish.

Figure 8.7 Different types of fish

Fish can be prepared by the chef or fishmonger. It can be cut into:

- fillets – a cut of fish that is free from bones
- steaks – thick slices of fish off the bone
- goujons – filleted fish that has been cut into strips.

Figure 8.8 Filleting a round fish

Eggs

- The term 'egg' applies to all edible eggs of birds such as hens, ducks, quail, geese and gulls. Hens' eggs are the eggs most commonly eaten in the UK.
- Eggs have three main parts: the shell, the white and the yolk.
- Eggs need to be removed from their shell before they can be used. Some recipes require a whole egg; others may need the egg separated into the white and the yolk.
- Egg whites can be whisked to form a foam. When preparing egg whites to be whisked it is important that there is no trace of yolk, and the bowl and whisk should be clean. If there are any traces of fat, the egg whites will not whisk.

Dairy products

- Milk from animals such as cows, sheep and goats is used to create dairy products. These include cream, cheese, yoghurt and butter.
- Dairy foods should be prepared on a white chopping board.

Milk

- There are many different types of milk, for example whole milk, semi-skimmed, skimmed, evaporated, UHT (ultra heat treated) and condensed.
- Soya, almond and coconut milks are useful for people who are lactose intolerant.
- When using milk in recipes, it is important to measure it accurately in order to get the correct consistency of mix.

Figure 8.9 Egg whites produce a foam when whisked

Cream

Milk contains butterfat; when butterfat is skimmed off the surface of the milk, it is known as cream. The choice of cream depends on its use:

- clotted cream is a thick, rich, creamy and spreadable cream; it is slightly granular in texture and cannot be whipped
- double cream is 48 per cent fat, so it can whip to one and a half times its original volume

- whipping cream is 38 per cent fat and can also be whipped
- single cream is 18 per cent fat and will not whip, so it is used in recipes or for pouring
- soured cream does not whip and is thick in texture.

Cheese

Cheese is made by adding an acidified bacterial culture and rennet to milk to create curds (solids) and whey (liquid). The whey is drained away and the curd is then made into cheese.

Cheese can be grouped into hard, semi-hard and soft:

- hard cheeses can be sliced and grated easily
- semi-hard cheeses can be grated, but are softer in texture
- soft cheeses are often used for cheeseboards or can be melted as part of a recipe.

Figure 8.10 A cheeseboard

Table 8.3 **Examples of hard, semi-hard and soft cheeses**

Hard cheese	Semi-hard cheese	Soft cheese
Cheddar	Wensleydale	Brie
Double Gloucester	Lancashire	Camembert
Red Leicester	Caerphilly	Dolcelatte
Parmesan	Edam	Cambozola
	Mozzarella	
	Stilton	

Curd cheese is made from pasteurised milk, which is soured by the addition of a milk-souring culture and rennet, which produces a soft, low-fat cheese.

- Cottage cheese is a low-fat, high-protein cheese.
- Quark is a salt-free, fat-free soft cheese.

Yoghurt

- Milk from cows, goats or ewes (sheep) can be used to make yoghurt.
- Yoghurt is made by adding a bacterial **starter culture** to milk.
- There are many different types of yoghurt, such as set, low-fat, luxury and flavoured.
- Yoghurt is mainly eaten as a snack or as part of a dessert.

> **Starter culture**: a small quantity of harmless bacteria that is used to start the fermentation of yoghurt or cheese.

Butter

Butter is made by churning cream. During this process the butterfat in the cream forms solids (butter) and the liquid (buttermilk) is drained off.

Cereals, flour, rice, pasta

- Cereals are cultivated grasses. The grains from the grasses are used as a food source.
- Most cereals are processed to form other foods or ingredients, for example flour, breakfast cereals, bread and pasta.

Table 8.4 Major cereal crops and their uses

Type of cereal	Use
Wheat	Ground into flour
Barley	Pearl barley, an alternative to rice
Rice	Used in main meals or as an accompaniment. Different types include white, brown, basmati, arborio
Oats	Ground into oatmeal, rolled into flakes
Corn (maize)	Boiled or steamed as a vegetable (corn on the cob, or sweetcorn)

Flour

Wheat is milled to make flour.

Table 8.5 Different types of flour

Type of flour	Description
Plain flour (soft flour)	All the bran and the wheatgerm are removed, leaving white flour
Self-raising flour (soft flour)	Plain flour with added raising agent (such as baking powder)
Strong flour	Flour made from wheat that contains a high amount of protein; it is used in bread making
Wholemeal flour	Contains all of the grain; nothing has been removed
Brown flour	Similar to wholemeal but the coarse bits are removed; high in dietary fibre

Pasta

- Pasta is a mixture of flour, salt and water; sometimes egg is added to enrich it. The word pasta literally means 'dough' or 'paste'.
- Pasta can be bought in many shapes and can be purchased dried or fresh. Some chefs – particularly in Italian restaurants – make their own pasta from double 00 (doppio zero) flour – a finely milled Italian flour.

Figure 8.11 Making pasta

Pasta dough

- 200 g double 00 flour
- ½ teaspoon of salt
- 1 tablespoon of oil
- 2 eggs
- 1–2 tablespoons of water

Method

1 Place the flour and salt on the work top and mix in the rest of the ingredients using your hands.
2 Knead the dough for five minutes or until it is smooth.
3 Leave it to rest for 30 minutes.
4 Use a pasta machine to roll the dough then cut it into the desired shape.

- Pasta machines make easy work of rolling and cutting pasta dough.
- Once you have a long, thin strip of dough it needs to be dried over a pasta dryer or a wooden pole before cutting or shaping it.
- If cutting the pasta by machine, the correct cutters need to be fitted. The shapes can also be cut by hand.
- A huge variety of shapes can be made out of pasta dough using a pasta machine.

Fruit and vegetables

Types of fruit include:

- soft fruits, for example raspberries and strawberries
- citrus fruits, for example oranges and lemons
- stone fruits, for example plums and peaches
- fleshy fruits, for example apples and pears
- vine fruits, for example grapes.

Types of vegetables include:

- fruit vegetables, for example tomatoes and peppers
- legumes, for example peas and beans
- flower vegetables, for example broccoli and globe artichokes
- leafy vegetables, for example spinach and chard
- stem vegetables, for example asparagus and celery
- fungi, for example mushrooms
- bulbs, for example onions and garlic
- roots, for example carrots and parsnips.

Figure 8.12 Selection of vegetables

Preparation of fruit and vegetables

Wash all fruit and vegetables before use. They can then be prepared using a number of techniques, as shown in Table 8.6. A brown chopping board should be used for the preparation of vegetables and a green chopping board should be used for salad and fruit.

Table 8.6 **Key terms in the preparation of fruit and vegetables**

Key term	Description
Mash	To reduce to a soft mass using a masher or ricer, for example using a masher to make mashed potato
Shred	To slice in long, thin strips, for example shredding cabbage to make coleslaw
Scissor snip	To cut food with a pair of scissors instead of a knife, for example using scissors to snip herbs into small pieces
Crush	To crush into tiny pieces with another implement, for example soft fruit can be crushed to make a textured sauce or decoration
Grate	To make coarse or fine threads by repeatedly rubbing it over the side of a grater (a grater has small, sharp-edged holes of different sizes and shapes), for example grating carrots or onions for a salad
Peel	To remove the skin of fruit and vegetables using a peeler, for example taking the skin off potatoes
Segment	To peel and divide into pieces, for example an orange or a grapefruit

Vegetables can be chopped or sliced into different shapes and sizes according to the dish they are being used for.

Table 8.7 **Vegetable cuts**

Vegetable cut	Description	
Julienne (matchstick strips)	1 Cut the vegetable into 2 cm lengths for short julienne; 4 cm lengths for long julienne. 2 Cut into thin slices lengthways. 3 Cut each slice into thin, even-sized strips.	
Brunoise (small dice)	To make small diced vegetables, cut each julienne strip into small dice	
Macédoine (medium dice)	1 Cut the vegetable into even-sized lengths. 2 Cut the length into 0.5 cm slices. 3 Cut each slice into 0.5 cm strips. 4 Cut the strips into 0.5 cm cubes.	
Jardinière (batons)	1 Cut the vegetables into 2.5 cm lengths. 2 Cut into 3 mm slices lengthways. 3 Cut the slices into batons.	

Soya products

- Soya beans (known as edamame beans when eaten fresh) are used in many products, including tofu and textured vegetable protein (TVP).
- TVP is very bland so it needs to be used with strong-flavoured ingredients.
- TVP is often purchased dried and needs to be rehydrated.
- Tofu is often marinated before cooking to add extra flavour. It can be cut into cubes, grilled or stir-fried.

Figure 8.13 Marinated tofu

Assessment tip

You will need to use a comprehensive range of techniques when preparing commodities for your dishes to get a Level 2 distinction in your internal assessment. The techniques you use should be carried out effectively, independently and with faultless speed and precision. Make sure you consider food safety at all times when preparing commodities.

Think about the techniques you could show when preparing different commodities and try to use a variety of these quickly and correctly in your dishes. For example:
- poultry – jointing a chicken
- meat – trimming fat from a lamb chop
- fish – filleting a piece of fish
- eggs – separating eggs to whisk the egg whites for a meringue
- dairy products – whipping cream to the correct consistency
- cereals – making pasta dough from doppio zero (00) flour
- fruit and vegetables – making sure they are peeled and cut correctly, for example julienne strips for a stir-fry
- soya products – tofu cut neatly into cubes or strips and marinated.

Typical mistake

Students sometimes use the incorrect piece of equipment when preparing commodities. Using the correct equipment will help to ensure you can prepare commodities quickly and with precision. For example, use a peeler to take the skin off a carrot, a balloon whisk when whipping cream, and a filleting knife when filleting fish.

Now test yourself

TESTED

1 State two reasons why you would sieve flour before making a cake.   (2 marks)
2 You have been asked to choose a selection of cheeses for a cheeseboard. Give two examples of each of the following types of cheese that would be suitable for a cheeseboard.   (6 marks)
    a) Hard cheese
    b) Semi-hard cheese
    c) Soft cheese
3 Identify two types of cream that can be whipped.   (2 marks)
4 Chicken is a popular meat, but it can sometimes lack flavour. Name three recipes that can enhance the flavour of chicken.   (3 marks)
5 Name the cream that is traditionally used on top of scones and jam.   (1 mark)

3.2 Assuring quality of commodities to be used in food preparation

It is essential that all commodities are quality checked before they are prepared and cooked.

- The quality of a commodity can be checked by sight, smell and touch.
- Commodities should be stored and packaged correctly to ensure they are safe to prepare, cook and eat.
- In all cases the date mark (**best before** and **use-by dates**) should be checked.

> **Best before date**: food is at its best quality before this date, although it is still safe to eat after this date.
>
> **Use-by date**: food must be consumed by this date to prevent food poisoning.

Poultry

REVISED

- Poultry should have a plump breast and firm flesh.
- It should be moist but not sticky to touch.
- The skin should be white and unbroken.
- It should smell fresh.

Storage

- Poultry has a short shelf life and should be eaten within a few days of purchase, or frozen.
- It should be covered and stored towards the bottom of the refrigerator, away from cooked meat, to avoid cross-contamination.

Figure 8.14 **A fresh chicken**

Packaging

Poultry can be bought fresh and, if not packaged, it should then be wrapped in greaseproof paper so that the air can circulate around it.

Meat

REVISED

- Fresh meat should not smell.
- Meat should have a firm, close texture.
- Meat should never be slimy; it should be moist.
- Meat should not have too much fat on it or contain too much **gristle**. The fat should be a pale creamy colour, not yellow.

> **Gristle**: tough and inedible tissue in meat.

Figure 8.15 **Fresh meat: shin of beef, belly pork and leg of lamb**

Storage

- Meat has a short shelf life and should be eaten within a few days of purchase, or frozen.
- It should be covered and stored towards the bottom of the refrigerator, away from cooked meat, to avoid cross-contamination.

Packaging

Meat can be bought fresh and, if not packaged, it should then be wrapped in greaseproof paper so that the air can circulate around it.

Fish

REVISED

- Fish should smell like the sea or have no aroma at all. If the smell is strongly fishy then the fish is not fresh. There should be no smell of ammonia.
- The fish should feel firm, not spongy; it should have a thin covering of slime and should not feel dry.
- Fish with scales should have an even coverage of scales; they should not be coming loose and there should not be patches without scales.
- The eyes of the fish should be bright, not sunken and dull.
- The gills should look red, not pale.

Figure 8.16 **Fresh trout**

Storage

Fish deteriorates very quickly, so it should be bought as fresh as possible. Once purchased, it should be cooked, chilled or frozen as soon as possible.

Packaging

Once it is bought it should be wrapped in paper for storage in the fridge. Fish can also be bought ready-packaged.

Eggs

REVISED

- There is no smell to an egg as it is surrounded by the shell. Once opened it will be obvious if it has gone off as it will smell rotten.
- The eggshell should be hard and smooth to touch.
- The egg should not have any cracks in the shell.

Storage

- Eggs are high-risk foods so should be stored in the fridge.
- Eggs should be stored with the pointed end downwards and should be kept away from strong-smelling foods.

Packaging

Eggs are usually sold in pre-packed boxes or trays.

Figure 8.17 **Packaged eggs**

Dairy products

REVISED

- Milk, cream and butter should smell fresh, not sour.
- Yoghurt should smell slightly acidic.
- As dairy products should be stored in a fridge, they should feel cold.
- Cheese should be checked for mould (unless it is blue cheese).

Answers and quick quizzes at www.hoddereducation.co.uk/myrevisionnotes

Storage

- Milk, yoghurt, cheese, cream and butter should be kept in the fridge, away from strong-smelling foods. Butter should be wrapped.
- Tinned milk should be stored in a dry store. Dried milk should be stored in an airtight container and kept in a dry store.

Packaging

- Dairy products are usually purchased in plastic containers – check the plastic is not cracked and check the use-by date.
- Cheese should be stored in its original packaging, and the wrapping sealed when opened.

Cereals, flour, rice, pasta

REVISED

- There is no smell to uncooked rice, pasta or flour.
- Dried pasta should be brittle; fresh pasta should feel softer to touch.
- Sometimes flour can contain insects so check there is no movement in the flour or that it has no black flecks if it has been stored for a long time.

Storage

- Cereals have a very long shelf life, but they are prone to infestation by insects if kept for long periods of time, particularly if they are not kept in a covered container. They should be kept in a cool, dry place.
- Fresh-made pasta becomes very brittle when it dries, so it should only be stored for 24 hours in a fridge in a plastic bag.

Packaging

Cereals are generally bought in packaging; once opened they are best transferred to an airtight container.

Fruit and vegetables

REVISED

- Fruit and vegetables should smell fresh.
- Fruit and vegetables should be firm or springy to the touch; they should not feel soggy.
- Fruit and vegetables should look shiny, have no mould, no bruises and should not be rotten.

Storage

- Fruit and vegetables should be stored in a cool, well-ventilated area or refrigerator.
- Salad vegetables should be stored in the refrigerator.
- Bananas should not be stored in the refrigerator.
- Most fruit should not be stored touching each other, otherwise it will soften and start to rot.

Packaging

Fruit and vegetables can be bought loose or in plastic packaging called a punnet. Soft fruits can be stored in punnets, but are better removed and placed in a single layer, not touching and can be wrapped in cling film.

Figure 8.18 Punnets of fruit

Soya products

- Tofu and TVP do not have a specific smell.
- Tofu is quite spongy and moist; TVP is usually sold as dried granules and is firm, or the granules are frozen.
- There should be no evidence of mould.

Storage

- TVP is made from soya bean flour. It can be bought dried or frozen, so it can be kept in the store cupboard or freezer.
- Tofu is made from ground soya beans. It is sold as a curd, usually from the chiller cabinet, so should be stored in the fridge.

Figure 8.19 Tofu

Packaging

Tofu and TVP are usually packaged in plastic, which should be checked to ensure it is all sealed. The use-by date should be checked.

Revision activity

Make yourself some quality standard cards on each commodity. Include information for each commodity on what it should look like and smell like, and how to store and package it.

Assessment tip

To get the highest mark in the internal assessment you have to demonstrate that you can check the quality of all the commodities you are using. So, you need to smell them, touch them, look at them, ensure they have been packaged correctly, stored correctly and check the use-by and best before dates. If any of them do not meet the quality requirements, then you will need to resolve this. For instance:
- if an egg is cracked, use another one
- check all the dates to ensure no commodity is out of date
- if a strawberry is soggy and bruised, do not use it
- keep all high-risk foods, such as meat, fish, eggs and dairy products, in the fridge
- keep all frozen food in the freezer and only get it out when you need to use it.

Typical mistake

Do not forget to check *all* your commodities for quality. If you don't check them all and your teacher has to give you guidance on this, you will get a lower level for this criterion.

Now test yourself

1 Describe how meat and poultry should be stored. (2 marks)
2 Name three points to look for when choosing fresh fish. (3 marks)
3 State how you should store cereals. (1 mark)
4 Explain how to ensure fresh raspberries bought in a punnet stay fresh for longer. (3 marks)
5 State two points you could use to check the quality of meat by touching it. (2 marks)

Answers and quick quizzes at **www.hoddereducation.co.uk/myrevisionnotes**

3.3 Techniques in cooking of commodities

Table 8.8 Common techniques used when cooking food

Method of cooking	Definition and information	Foods suitable for cooking by this method
Baking	Cooking food in a hot oven without extra fat being added	Cakes, biscuits, scones, pastry, vegetables, fish, puddings, desserts, fruit and pre-prepared products
Blanching	Food is cooked very quickly in boiling water then cooled quickly to stop the cooking process	Fruit and vegetables are blanched before freezing to help keep their colour and to destroy enzymes that would cause them to spoil
Boiling	Foods are cooked in boiling water, milk or stock, which makes them tender	Older, tougher (and therefore cheaper) cuts of meat, for example shin of beef, whole eggs, gammon, rice, and pasta
Braising	A moist method used for cooking larger pieces of food; the food is cooked slowly in liquid (usually stock) for a long time in a pan, on a very low temperature Food can be braised either on the hob or in the oven	Meat, vegetables and rice
Deep-fat frying	Small tender pieces of food are immersed in very hot fat for a short period of time	Meat, poultry, vegetables, fish, fruit, onion bhajis, churros, doughnuts
Dry frying	Cooking food on a low heat without any fat or oil	Foods that naturally contain fat, for example bacon and sausages
Grilling (griddling)	Cooking food by applying heat to its surface	Smaller cuts of meat, vegetables, fish, breads
Poaching	Food is cooked very gently in a liquid that is just below boiling point	Chicken, fish, eggs and fruit, for example pears
Roasting	Cooking and browning with the aid of fat	Meat, vegetables
Sautéing	To cook in fat or shallow fry	Chicken, potatoes
Shallow frying	A small amount of fat is used to cook food in a frying pan	Eggs, burgers, fishcakes, sausages, bacon
Steaming	Food is cooked by the steam coming off boiling water	Potatoes, vegetables, sponge puddings, fish
Stir-frying	Small pieces of food are fried quickly in a small amount of oil in a wok	Steak, chicken breast, vegetables, noodles

Figure 8.20 Steaming is considered a very healthy method of cooking

Table 8.9 Other techniques used during the cooking process

Technique	Definition and information
Chilling	Chilling is a process that helps stop harmful bacteria from growing. Chilled food should be kept in the fridge between 0 °C and 5 °C to keep them safe, for example: ● food with a use-by date ● cooked dishes ● other ready-to-eat food such as prepared salads and desserts.
Cooling	Food that is not going to be eaten straight away is cooled to be eaten cold or to be reheated later. Food should be cooled within 90 minutes to 5 °C or below to keep it out of the temperature danger zone. Blast chillers cool food rapidly by moving very cold air around the food.
Hot holding	Hot holding is keeping cooked food hot at a minimum temperature of 63 °C.

Poultry

REVISED ☐

● Poultry is cooked to improve its texture by making it tender and digestible, and to ensure any harmful bacteria that may cause food poisoning are killed.

● The method of cooking selected will depend on the type and cut of poultry.

Table 8.10 shows the method of cooking, and the type and cut suited to it.

Table 8.10 Methods used when cooking poultry

Method of cooking	Type and cut of poultry suitable
Grilling	Tender cuts of meat, for example breast
Shallow frying	Chicken breasts or thighs can be cut into strips and fried using a small amount of oil
Roasting	Whole chicken, turkey

Recipe suggestions

● Roast chicken

● Chicken fricassée

● Chicken and ham pie

● Chicken curry

● Chicken Kiev

Figure 8.21 A roast chicken

Serving advice

● Roast chicken or turkey is traditionally served with bread sauce, bacon-wrapped chipolata sausages, and cranberry sauce.

● Chicken is low in fat and can be quite dry, so it is often cooked in a sauce.

● Chicken is white in colour so should be accompanied by colourful foods or garnished.

Meat

- Meat is cooked to improve its texture by making it tender and digestible.
- The method of cooking selected will depend on the type and cut of meat.

Table 8.11 shows the method of cooking, and the type and cut of meat suited to it.

Table 8.11 Methods used when cooking meat

Method of cooking	Type and cut of meat suitable
Grilling	Tender cuts of meat, for example chops, bacon, gammon, steak
Shallow frying	Tender cuts of meat; meat such as steak can be cut into strips and fried using a small amount of oil
Roasting	Topside, silverside, leg or shoulder of lamb, belly pork, leg of pork
Braising	Brisket, breast or shoulder of lamb, belly or shoulder of pork
Stewing	Shin of beef, gammon

Recipe suggestions

- Beef stroganoff
- Steak and ale pie
- Beef Wellington
- Lamb tagine
- Beef olives
- Goulash

Figure 8.22 Beef olives

Serving advice

- Roast beef is traditionally served with Yorkshire pudding and horseradish sauce.
- Beef stews are traditionally served with dumplings.
- Lamb is traditionally served with mint sauce.
- Pork is a rich meat so it is traditionally served with apple sauce, which can counteract the richness of the pork. Sage and onion stuffing is often served with pork.

Fish

- Fish cooks very easily and is easy to digest. This also means that care needs to be taken when cooking because overcooking will result in the fish falling apart.
- Cooking improves colour and flavour and destroys harmful bacteria.
- Different types of fish are suited to different cooking methods.

Table 8.12 lists the types of fish and seafood, and how they can be cooked.

Table 8.12 Methods used for cooking different types of fish

Type of fish	How it can be cooked
White fish	
Cod/pollack	Cut into steaks or filleted into portions; it is usually fried or poached
Haddock	Fried, poached or smoked
Halibut	Poached, boiled, grilled or shallow fried; it can also be smoked
Monkfish	Pan-fried or baked
Plaice	Deep-fried or grilled
Sea bass	Baked whole
Oily fish	
Herring	Grilled, fried or soused
Kippers	Split, salted, dried or smoked as herrings
Mackerel	Grilled, fried, smoked or soused
Salmon	Poached, pan-fried, baked, smoked
Sardines	Cooked whole, often pan-fried
Trout	Stuffed and baked, poached, grilled or fried; it can also be smoked
Tuna	Grilled as steaks or pan-fried
Whitebait	Deep-fried whole
Shellfish	
Cockles	Steamed or boiled
Mussels	Steamed or boiled
Oysters	Mostly eaten raw
Scallops	Pan-fried in butter or oil
Lobster	Boiled or steamed; it can also be baked
Prawns	Stir-fried, grilled, boiled or steamed
Crab	Boiled

Raw fish is eaten all around the world; if fish is to be eaten raw it should be very fresh and finely sliced, for example sushi.

Table 8.13 Specific points to note when cooking fish

Method of cooking	Notes
Frying	Coating fish keeps the flavour in and protects its delicate structure; fish can be coated in egg and breadcrumbs, batter or just flour and fried
Grilling/barbecuing	This method conserves the flavour and is really successful with whole fish, flat fish and oily fish; the fish should be turned only once to ensure it does not fall apart
Baking	Fish can be baked, particularly if stuffed, or wrapped in foil or parchment to preserve flavour and retain moisture
Poaching	Fish should be poached in a small amount of liquid; to retain nutrients lost in the cooking liquid, it can be used as the basis of a sauce to serve with the fish
Steaming	Fish can be steamed very successfully in an electric steamer or on a lightly greased plate over a pan of boiling water

Recipe suggestions

- Fish goujons
- Salmon fingers
- Seafood chowder
- Paella
- Fish pie
- Stuffed sea bass

Figure 8.23 Fish goujons

Serving advice

Fish can sometimes lack colour and flavour. This can be improved by:

- adding flavour to the fish – frying in butter, adding a batter or breadcrumbs
- serving fish with a sauce – white sauce in a fish pie, tartare sauce with grilled fish
- using colourful garnishes such as parsley, tomatoes and lemon slices
- choosing colourful vegetables to accompany the fish – broccoli, sweetcorn, green beans.

Eggs

REVISED

Table 8.14 How eggs are used in cooking

Use	Examples of dishes
Coagulation: when eggs are heated, the protein in the white and yolk starts to coagulate (set)	Boiled eggs, poached eggs, fried eggs, scrambled eggs and omelettes
Thickening: adding egg and heating; this also enriches the sauce by adding extra nutrients	Sauces, custards, soups
Binding: eggs bind two or more ingredients together and add moisture; as the food is cooked, the egg coagulates and keeps the product whole	Rissoles, burgers, meatballs, croquettes
Coating: eggs are used as coating, for example egg and breadcrumbs; the egg enables the coating to stick to the surface of a product and forms a protective barrier during cooking	Chicken goujons, fish fingers, Scotch eggs
Glazing: egg can be brushed over the surface of a baked item before it is cooked to give the product a glossy, golden-brown finish	Scones and pastry products such as pies, pasties and sausage rolls
Garnishing: slices of hard-boiled egg can be used as a garnish	Kedgeree, curry
Emulsification: egg yolk can be used to stabilise emulsions; adding egg yolk to a mixture of oil and water prevents the two liquids from separating	Mayonnaise
Foaming: when egg white is whisked it incorporates air and produces a foam; the whole egg can also be whisked to give fatless sponges a light and airy texture	Meringues, soufflés, mousses; used in Swiss roll, sponge flan and sponge cake

Recipe suggestions

- Quiche Lorraine
- Baked egg custard
- Roulade
- Meringue
- Lemon curd
- Mayonnaise

Figure 8.24 Eggs Benedict

Serving advice

- Egg dishes can be served as meals, such as quiche Lorraine, accompanied by a salad or jacket potatoes and vegetables.
- Eggs used in baked products such as cakes, which can be decorated to enhance their appearance.

Dairy products

REVISED

Cream

Table 8.15 **Different types of cream and their uses**

Type of cream	Uses
Soured cream	Dips and as a topping for jacket potatoes
Single cream	An accompaniment to desserts, or added to sauces or soups to enrich them
Whipping cream	Whipped and piped in sweet dishes; can also be used as a filling for cakes and pastries
Double cream	Poured over desserts or added to sauces; it can also float on the top of coffee; whipped and piped as a decoration on cakes and desserts
Clotted cream	Traditionally served as part of a cream tea with scones, jam and a pot of tea

Recipe suggestions

- Crème brûlée
- Potatoes dauphinoise
- Piped whipped cream on a gateau
- Cream tea – scones, jam and clotted cream
- Panna cotta
- Mousse

Serving advice

Cream can be served separately to complement some desserts. When piped it looks attractive and can enhance the appearance of some dishes.

Cheese

Table 8.16 Different types of cheese and their uses

Type of cheese	Uses
Hard cheeses such as Cheddar	Cauliflower cheese, pasta bakes
Brie, Cheddar, Edam, soft cheeses	Fillings for sandwiches, paninis, jacket potatoes
Cottage cheese, cream cheese	Dips and spreads
Cheddar, mozzarella	Baked products – cheese twists, quiche, pizza
Mascarpone	Desserts – tiramisu, cheesecake
Emmental	Fondue

Recipe suggestions

- Cauliflower cheese
- Cheesecake
- Carrot cake with cream cheese frosting
- Fondue
- Cheese and potato pie

Figure 8.25 Cheesecake

Serving advice

Cheese can be eaten in its natural form. A cheeseboard is served in a restaurant as either a fourth course or as an alternative to dessert.

Milk

Whole milk, semi-skimmed, skimmed and UHT milk can be used in many ways, for example:

- soups – cream of mushroom
- sauces – parsley sauce, all-in-one or roux sauce
- batters – pancakes, Yorkshire puddings
- puddings – rice pudding, bread and butter pudding
- baked products – bread, scones and cakes
- hot drinks – added to coffee, tea, lattes, cappuccinos, hot chocolate
- cold drinks – milkshakes, smoothies
- glazing – brushing over the surface of foods to give a smooth, shiny finish.

In addition:

- Soya milk is a very useful alternative to cows' milk and can be used by vegetarians, vegans and people with an intolerance of cows' milk.
- Goats' milk is nutritionally similar to cows' milk and has a very distinctive taste. It is useful for people who are allergic to cows' milk.
- Evaporated milk and condensed milk are used in desserts and baking for recipes such as rice pudding, banoffee pie and millionaire's shortbread.

Recipe suggestions

- Pancakes
- Mushroom soup
- Lattes
- Scones
- Milk puddings, such as rice pudding

Yoghurt

There are many types of yoghurt available to use in cooking.

- Stirred yoghurt has a smooth fluid consistency.
- Set yoghurt has a more solid and firmer texture.
- Low-fat yoghurts and whole milk creamy yoghurts are available both plain and flavoured.
- Yoghurt drinks are also increasing in popularity; some contain 'friendly' bacteria that helps the digestive system.

Recipe suggestions

- Drinks: smoothies and milkshakes can be made with yoghurt and fruit.
- Desserts: yoghurt can be used when making cheesecake or mousse.
- Salad dressings: yoghurt, particularly low-fat yoghurt, is useful when making salad dressings and dips.
- Cream or cream fillings.
- Toppings: on cereals, combined with herbs or other ingredients as a topping for jacket potatoes.

Serving advice

Yoghurt can be used as a topping or part of a dip.

Butter

Butter can be used in many different ways and adds colour and flavour to a range of dishes.

Recipe suggestions

- Spreading: on bread, toast and crumpets.
- As a base: for sauces and soups, making brandy butter, butter icing.
- Pastry: shortcrust, sweet shortcrust, puff, flaky.
- Shallow frying, but care needs to be taken because it burns at high temperatures.
- Basting: melted butter on fish or meat; can be combined with herbs or spices.
- Glazing: cooked food such as potatoes and carrots.

Serving advice

- Butter acts as a protective layer in sandwiches, preventing the moist filling making the bread soggy.
- Butter pats or curls can be served with bread rolls to accompany a meal.

Cereals

Table 8.17 Different cereals and their uses

Type of cereal	Uses
Wheat	Ground to make flour, which is used in bread, biscuits, cakes, pastry, sauces and batters
	Durum wheat is used to make doppio zero (00) flour, which is used to make pasta
	Couscous is steamed, dried and cracked grains of durum wheat
	Wheat flakes are also added to breakfast cereals
Rye	Used to make bread and crispbreads
Barley	Pearl barley thickens soups, stews and casseroles
	Barley is also used in the production of barley water
	Malt extract and malt flour is made from barley and is used to make malt loaf
	Beer is also made from barley
Oats	Rolled oats are used for porridge, muesli and flapjacks
	Ground oatmeal is used to make biscuits such as oatcakes and digestive biscuits
Corn	It is eaten as sweetcorn and corn on the cob
	It is the main constituent in cornflakes
	Can be converted to glucose syrup or corn syrup

Flour

Table 8.18 Different types of flour and their uses

Type of flour	Uses
Plain flour (soft flour)	Cakes, sauces, biscuits and pastries
Self-raising flour (soft flour)	Sponge cakes, scones and puddings
Strong flour	Bread, Yorkshire pudding, puff pastry and choux pastry
Brown flour	Breads, pastries and biscuits
Wholemeal flour	Breads, pastries and biscuits

Rice

- Rice can be cooked by boiling, steaming, frying, stewing, braising and baking.
- Use a large amount of water when boiling rice.
- Rice is a high-risk food once cooked, and reheating should be avoided.

Table 8.19 Different types of rice and their uses

Type of rice	Uses
Short grain rice	Rounded grains that tend to stick together; used for sweet dishes such as rice pudding
Long grain rice	The most popular type of rice as it has many uses, for example as an accompaniment to dishes such as chilli con carne, or as an alternative to pasta or potatoes
Arborio rice	A round grain used to make risotto
Brown rice	Available as short grain and long grain rice Takes longer to cook because it contains the bran Healthier than other types of rice, but it can be used in the same way as long grain rice

Basmati rice Dark wild rice Risotto rice

Parboiled long grain rice Rose matta rice Red cargo rice

Figure 8.26 Different types of rice

Pasta

- Pasta should always be cooked in a large pan of water; salt should also be added. The water should always come to the boil before the pasta is added.
- Ideally, two litres of water should be used for 350 g of pasta, so a large pan is useful – this allows space for the pasta to move around.
- Oil can be added to the water, which helps to stop the water from frothing up and over the pan; it also helps to stop the pasta from sticking together.
- Once the pasta has been added to the boiling water it needs to come back to the boil – calculate the cooking time from this point.
- Once cooked, pasta should be **al dente** – firm to the bite – and should be drained thoroughly before serving.

Recipe suggestions

- Spaghetti carbonara
- Spaghetti Bolognese
- Lasagne
- Ravioli
- Cannelloni
- Risotto

- Flapjacks
- Bread
- Cakes
- Scones
- Biscuits

Figure 8.27 Lasagne

Serving advice

The Eatwell Guide says that meals should be based on starchy carbohydrate foods such as cereals. Cereal products are often eaten as an accompaniment to a main meal.

Fruit and vegetables

Fruit and vegetables can be eaten raw or cooked. Vegetables should be cooked quickly in order to retain as many nutrients as possible. Generally, they are either:

- boiled
- steamed
- baked.

Figure 8.28 Stuffed pepper

Recipe suggestions

- Apple pie
- Tarte Tatin
- Mousse
- Lemon cheesecake
- Fruit flan
- Fruit tartlets
- Fruit coulis

- Stir-fry
- Duchesse potatoes
- Cauliflower cheese
- Coleslaw
- Stuffed peppers
- Ratatouille

Serving advice

- Many vegetables are served as an accompaniment to a main meal. They should complement the main meal in terms of colour and texture.
- Vegetables can also be made into complete dishes such as stir-fries, soups and casseroles.
- Both vegetables and fruit can be used to garnish or decorate a dish.

Soya products

Soya products need some flavour added before they are cooked as they can be quite bland. This can be done by the addition of herbs and spices, strong flavours such as chilli, or by marinating.

Figure 8.29 Crispy deep-fried tofu

Recipe suggestions

- TVP is used mainly as a meat extender – this means that less meat is used in a dish as the TVP replaces part of it. It can be used in casseroles, stews, pies and pasties.
- Marinated tofu is used in wraps and stir-fries.

Serving advice

Tofu should be garnished or served with colourful accompaniments because it can be bland in both texture and colour.

Now test yourself

TESTED ☐

1 Explain why dry frying is a healthier method of cooking than shallow frying. (1 mark)
2 State which of the following meats you would grill. (1 mark)
   a) Whole chicken
   b) Shin of beef
   c) Lamb shanks
   d) Steak
3 Describe the term 'roasting'. (1 mark)
4 Describe how white fish can be cooked to make it more colourful and more flavoursome. (6 marks)
5 Name three foods for which poaching is a suitable cooking method. (3 marks)

3.4 Completing dishes using presentation techniques

Portion control

REVISED ☐

Portion size or **portion control** means controlling the size or quantity of food to be served to each customer. Portion control is essential in a catering business to ensure customers are happy and that the business makes a profit.

Controlling portion sizes will ensure that:

- there is little wastage of food, which keeps costs down
- customers have a consistent quantity of food, which will stop complaints about size of portions
- food items of the same size will take the same time to cook.

There are a number of ways in which portion size can be controlled:

- using scales to weigh foods such as steak
- using tools and equipment, for example using a scoop for ice cream, sorbet or mashed potato; using fruit juice glasses for measured drinks; using individual dishes for pies and desserts
- marking the surface of a cake or dessert into sections so it is easy to see where to cut it accurately
- using fruit such as strawberries to indicate portion size, for example one strawberry is equal to one portion
- counting food where appropriate, for example the number of biscuits for cheese and biscuits.

Figure 8.30 Using a scoop to measure a portion of ice cream

Table 8.20 Standard portions per person

Food	Amount per portion
Steak	120–250 g
Trout	1 whole fish
Soup	125 ml
Potatoes	125 g
Salmon	200 g

Position on serving dish

REVISED

There are many techniques you can use to present food attractively when plating up food for serving. It is important to consider the following:

- the serving dish and how the food will be placed on the dish
- use the centre height of the dish – a mound of food will look more attractive than if it is flattened on a plate or serving dish
- if laying out a plate of biscuits or canapés, arrange them in contrasting rows, as these look attractive
- overlap food such as fruit slices or slices of meat – it stops the food looking flat and dull on the plate
- keep colours to a minimum as lots of different colours can be overbearing; using two colours or different shades of a single colour works very successfully
- a sauce can be used to present food effectively, either by pouring it over the food, drizzling it, dotting it or serving it in a small jug alongside the food
- savoury food is often plated on oval dishes or plates; sweet food is often plated on round dishes or plates
- cakes and biscuits can be placed on a doily, then a plate, or on a tiered cake stand.

When plating up food to be served, particularly roast meals, the classical plating style can be used. This method of styling uses the idea of a plate being a clock:

- vegetables are between 12 and 3
- starchy foods are between 9 and 12
- the main component of the meal is between 3 and 9.

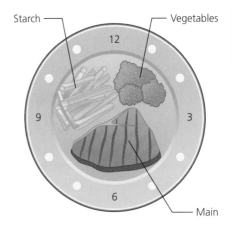

Figure 8.31 Plating food

Garnishes

Food needs to look attractive to a customer. There are a variety of ways a chef can be creative and make food look attractive. Adding a food to a finished dish can improve its appearance.

- Decorations on savoury food dishes are called **garnishes**.
- Decorations on sweet foods are simply called **decorations**.

Figure 8.32 A melon used creatively for a fruit salad

Figure 8.33 A strawberry fan

Table 8.21 Garnishes and decorations

Garnish/decoration name	Description
Fanning	A strawberry can be cut into slices with a knife leaving the top of the strawberry intact, which creates a fan effect
'Waterlily' effect	Using a knife, a V-shape is cut out around the middle to create a toothed effect; tomatoes and melon can be prepared in this way
Scoring with a fork	Score down with a sharp knife or fork to give ridged effect; cucumber and lemons can be prepared in this way
Twists	Slice, then cut from the edge to just past the centre; cucumber, oranges and lemons can be prepared in this way
Ribbons	Courgettes or cucumbers can be peeled along their length to produce ribbons that can be arranged in different ways, for example making a spiral, folding or wrapping round another food
Curls	Placing cut vegetables in ice-cold water can be very effective: ● radishes can be cut through almost to the base and will open out in iced water ● the green leaves of spring onions can be cut into small strips while still attached to the root; they will curl if left in iced water

Creative techniques

Many creative techniques can be used to enhance the appearance of food.

Table 8.22 Creative techniques used to enhance the appearance of food

Technique	Explanation
Blending	Mixing two or more ingredients together
Coulis	A thick sauce made from puréed cooked or raw fruit
Creaming	Slowly simmering a food such as spinach, or poaching it in milk or cream; it is then spooned, or shaped, and used as an accompaniment to a dish
Cutting and stencilling	A stencil can be used to create elaborate designs on cakes and biscuits, which can then be cut into the correct shape
Decorative glazes	Used to give a shiny appearance to desserts and cakes
Decorative icing	Used to enhance the appearance of a cake, small cakes and biscuits
	Different types of icing include glacé icing, fondant icing, royal icing, butter icing and chocolate ganache
	Royal icing and butter icing can be piped using nozzles to create many decorative effects
Dressings	Sauces prepared for salads; they add flavour and shine
Fluting	Pressing a decorative pattern in the edge of a pie crust before it is baked; it is sometimes called crimping
Foams	Foams are aerated liquids; the consistency of the foam will depend on the thickness of the liquid and the ratio of liquid to air
	A lighter foam is sometimes described as froth – such as on the top of a cappuccino – while a denser foam will look like a mousse
	Whipped cream, meringue and mousse are all foams
Glazing	Making a shiny surface on the food
Jus	A thin gravy or sauce that can be made from the juices of meat
Latticing	Creating a criss-cross pattern of strips in the preparation of various foods
Layering	Placing different foods on top of one another to create an attractive combination
Moulding	Food can be moulded into a shape by manipulating it
	Food can also be placed in a mould and then turned out
	A quenelle is an egg-shaped portion of food; it is made by shaping a soft, smooth food using two spoons
Piping	Pressing a soft food through a piping bag fitted with a shaped nozzle to form the food into an interesting shape
Shaping	Modelling food to create an attractive form

LO3 Be able to cook dishes

Figure 8.34 A creatively presented dessert

Figure 8.35 Piped duchesse potatoes

Now test yourself

TESTED ☐

1 State two reasons why it is important to portion meals correctly. **(2 marks)**
2 Name two foods that could be served using a scoop for correct portion control. **(2 marks)**
3 Describe techniques you could use to plate up your dishes attractively. **(6 marks)**
4 Describe a 'quenelle'. **(2 marks)**
5 Explain how to make a waterlily from a tomato. **(2 marks)**

3.5 Using food safety practices

Food hygiene and safety are very important when preparing food to protect customers from **food contamination**, which may cause **food poisoning**.

Personal hygiene

REVISED ☐

Rules for personal hygiene in the kitchen:

- Do not cough or sneeze near food.
- Do not touch your head, especially your mouth, nose and ears.
- You must wear a clean apron/chefs' whites when working with food because your own clothes will have bacteria on them. Wearing protective clothing stops bacteria on your clothes getting on to food.
- Footwear should be non-slip, flat and comfortable. No open-toes shoes, for example sandals.
- Do not brush your hair when wearing protective clothing or in any food areas.
- Long hair should be tied back and covered, or a hat/hair net should be worn.
- Cuts and scratches should be covered with a blue waterproof plaster.
- Do not prepare food if you are unwell with a tummy bug or cough/cold, as you could spread bacteria to food.

Handwashing

- Hands should be washed with soap and hot water regularly.
- Correct hand washing should take about 20 seconds.
- Make sure you wash your thumbs and fingertips.
- Rinse thoroughly then dry with a disposable cloth or hot air drier.

Work surfaces

Work surfaces should be thoroughly cleaned before you start preparing food, during preparation and cooking, and at the end.

Preparation and cooking of commodities

- Check the food is within the date marks – look carefully at the **best before** and **use-by dates**.
- Check the packaging is undamaged.
- Raw and cooked food should be kept separately to prevent the spread of bacteria.
- Commodities should be prepared on the correct coloured chopping boards.
- Fruit and vegetables should be washed and trimmed before serving to prevent contamination from the soil.
- Food should be reheated or cooked to a **core temperature** of 75 °C or above.
- Some foods should be turned or stirred during cooking to ensure even cooking.
- Visual checks can also be used to see if food is cooked – for example, chicken juices should run clear, sausages and burgers should be cooked through with no pink or red in the centre.
- A temperature probe can be used to check food is cooked in the centre. Clean and disinfect the probe before and after each use. Insert the probe into the thickest part of the food and wait for the reading to settle – this will be the core temperature.
- High-risk foods may be served chilled, at room temperature or hot.
  - ○ Chilled food should be served from the fridge.
  - ○ Food served at room temperature may be kept above the legal maximum fridge temperature as long as it is for a single period of up to four hours. After four hours the food should either be thrown away or chilled and kept at this temperature until eaten.
  - ○ Food served hot should be kept at 63 °C or above for no more than two hours.
- Use clean equipment when serving food; use tongs or spoons to handle food rather than hands.

> **Core temperature**: the temperature in the middle of the food.

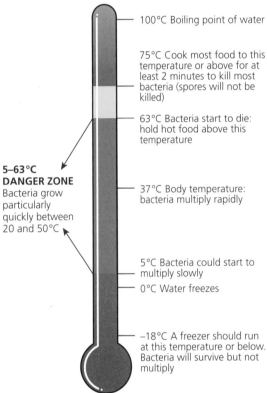

5–63 °C DANGER ZONE Bacteria grow particularly quickly between 20 and 50 °C

100 °C Boiling point of water

75 °C Cook most food to this temperature or above for at least 2 minutes to kill most bacteria (spores will not be killed)

63 °C Bacteria start to die: hold hot food above this temperature

37 °C Body temperature: bacteria multiply rapidly

5 °C Bacteria could start to multiply slowly

0 °C Water freezes

–18 °C A freezer should run at this temperature or below. Bacteria will survive but not multiply

Figure 8.36 Key temperatures in food safety

Figure 8.37 Using a food temperature probe to check beef burgers are thoroughly cooked

Chopping boards

Different coloured nylon chopping boards are used for different preparation tasks:

- a **green** board is used for salad and fruit
- a **brown** board is used for vegetables
- a **red** board is used for raw meat and chicken
- a **blue** board is used for raw fish
- a **yellow** board is used for cooked meat
- a **white** board is used for bread and dairy products.

Figure 8.38 Colour-coded chopping boards

Use of equipment

REVISED

- The fridge and freezer you are using must be at the correct temperatures:
  - fridge temperatures should be between 0 °C and 5 °C
  - freezer temperatures should be −18 °C or below.
- Ensure that high-risk foods are stored in the fridge, and frozen food in the freezer, until they are needed. If food needs to be chilled quickly, a blast chiller can be used.
- The bin you are using should have a lid.
- Equipment must be washed and disinfected between uses.
- Disposable gloves or tongs should be used to ensure food is handled as little as possible.
- Follow safety instructions for any equipment that you are using.
- Oven gloves should always be used when putting food in the oven and taking it out.
- Take care that pan handles are always pointing inwards.

Knives

- Make sure the knife is kept sharp – it causes fewer accidents.
- Use the right sized knife for the food you are cutting.
- When carrying a knife, always carry it by the handle with the point downwards.
- Always clean the knife after use to avoid cross-contamination.
- Always store knives carefully in a block or a wrap.

> **Revision activity**
>
> You should learn the safety rules for buying, storing, preparing, cooking and serving food thoroughly. You can then apply this knowledge to the practical assessment.

> **Assessment tip**
>
> To get a high mark in your internal assessment you need to use food safety practices effectively in preparation, cooking and completion. Your teacher should not have to intervene at all.

> **Typical mistake**
>
> Do not forget basic hygiene and safety procedures – you must use them at all times. Don't forget or cut corners as you work through your practical assessment, as this could lose you valuable marks.

Now test yourself

TESTED

1. Explain why food hygiene and safety are very important. (2 marks)
2. State six rules for personal hygiene. (6 marks)
3. State the main reason for wearing protective clothing in a catering kitchen. (1 mark)
4. State the correct temperatures (in °C) for each of the following. (4 marks)
   a) Fridge
   b) Freezer
   c) Cooking and reheating food
   d) Hot hold temperature
5. Describe how to use a temperature probe correctly. (3 marks)

Glossary

Ambient temperature: normal room temperature.

Amino acids: the building blocks of proteins.

Anaemia: a condition that affects the red blood cells in the body; it reduces the amount of oxygen that can be carried in the blood, leading to fatigue and breathlessness.

Anaphylactic shock: a severe allergic reaction that can be fatal.

Appetising: food that appeals to your senses.

Artificial fertilisers: man-made chemicals that increase the yield of crops.

Bacterium: a single bacteria.

Barista: makes and serves hot and cold drinks, especially coffee.

Beriberi: a disease caused by a lack of vitamin B1; it causes inflammation of the nerves and heart failure.

Best before date: food is at its best quality before this date, although it is still safe to eat after this date.

Beverage: a drink other than water.

Binary fission: the process by which bacteria reproduce by splitting into two.

Bistro: a small, relaxed French-style restaurant; prices are generally cheaper than a restaurant.

Budgeting skills: skills of managing money by prioritising essential spending before optional spending.

Bullying and harassment: when someone constantly finds fault with someone else and criticises them, often publicly; bullying tends to consist of small incidents over a long period of time, whereas harassment is often one or two serious incidents.

Business: a company that is smaller than a corporation.

Captive market: markets in which consumers can only choose between a limited number of suppliers; their only choice is to purchase what is available or to make no purchase at all.

Carbon footprint: a measure of the impact humans have on the environment in terms of the amount of greenhouse gases produced by a particular product or industry.

Catering: providing food and drinks services to customers.

Cholesterol: a fatty substance found in the blood; it is essential for humans but too much can be harmful.

Chopping: to cut food into small pieces of roughly the same size.

Coeliac: a person who has coeliac disease.

Coeliac disease: an autoimmune disease caused by a reaction of the immune system to gluten.

Commercial establishment: a business that provides food and drinks in order to make profit.

Components of dishes: ingredients already combined together; they can be purchased this way, such as ready-made pastry, or partly prepared by the chef, for example washed and drained salad ready for use.

Confectionery: sweets and chocolate.

Contract: a formal document outlining the role and responsibilities of a job that is designed to protect both the employee and employer.

Contract caterer: caterer supplying food and drinks at a venue where catering facilities are not available.

Control: a way of reducing the risk of a hazard causing harm.

Core temperature: the temperature in the middle of the food.

Coronary heart disease: the heart's blood supply is blocked or interrupted by a build-up of fatty substances in the coronary arteries.

Corporate: relating to a large business (corporation).

Cross-contamination: bacteria spreading from another place to another, for example from hands, work surfaces and utensils to food, or from raw meat to cooked meat.

Dairy products: milk from mammals (usually cows) as well as foods made from milk, such as yoghurt, cheese, cream and butter.

Danger zone: temperatures between 5 and 63 °C, which allow the rapid growth of bacteria.

Decorating: finishing off dishes before serving, for example piping cream on gateaux.

Decorations: decorations on sweet foods are simply called decorations.

Dehydration: when your body loses more water than you take in.

Demographics: statistical information about the population, for example age, gender and income.

Diabetes: a condition where the body's sugar levels cannot be controlled properly.

Discrimination: the unjust treatment of people, especially on the grounds of race, age or sex.

Dormant: a period of inactivity when bacteria are unable to multiply.

Dormitory accommodation: a large sleeping room containing several beds.

Dovetailing: preparing part of one dish and then part of another dish before the first dish is finished.

Dress code: a set of rules outlining the clothing that needs to be worn by people.

Drive-throughs: type of service that allows customers to purchase products without leaving their cars.

Due diligence: reasonable precautions that should be taken to ensure that a business complies with the law.

Eatwell Guide: government recommendations on eating healthily and achieving a balanced diet.

Enforcement action: action required by law following an inspection from an EHO.

Environmental Health Officer (EHO): responsible for inspecting all premises involved in food production to ensure that health and safety hazards are minimised.

Equality: being equal, especially in status, rights or opportunities.

Ethical: making choices based on opinions of right and wrong.

Farm to fork: a system that allows food to be traced back to its original source.

Fat-soluble vitamins: vitamins that dissolve in fat, for example vitamins A, D, E and K.

Fibre: a type of indigestible carbohydrate needed to help the body get rid of waste.

FIFO: first in, first out policy – used to ensure that older stock is used up first.

Fixed costs: costs that are always the same, for example rent and energy.

Fixed seats: seating that is permanently fixed to the floor.

Food contamination: food containing an additional substance that should not be there, for example bacteria.

Food intolerance: a sensitivity to certain foods; can cause symptoms such as nausea, abdominal pain, joint aches and pains, tiredness and weakness.

Food miles: the distance food has to travel from where it is grown, reared or caught to reach the consumer.

Food poisoning: an illness caused by eating contaminated food.

Food provenance: knowing where our food has come from and knowing how ingredients are grown, reared and caught and then transported to us.

Food safety plan: practical steps to identify and control hazards in order to establish and maintain food safety.

Gap in the market: an unmet consumer demand.

Garnishes: decorations on savoury food dishes.

Greenhouse gases: gases that trap heat and raise the Earth's temperature, for example carbon dioxide, methane and nitrous oxide.

Gristle: tough and inedible tissue in meat.

Gross profit: the amount of money made when the cost of goods (food and drink) sold has been deducted.

Growth spurt: a rapid increase in height.

Hazard: something that can cause harm.

Hazard analysis and critical control point (HACCP): a food safety process in which every step in the manufacture, storage and distribution of a food product is analysed to ensure that the food is safe to eat.

Health: being free from illness or injury.

Health and safety policy statement: a written statement by an employer of its commitment to health and safety for employees and the public.

High biological value (HBV) proteins: proteins that contain all ten essential amino acids, for example eggs and fish.

High blood pressure: a higher than normal force of blood pressing against the arteries.

High-risk foods: foods in which bacteria grow rapidly.

Hospitality: providing accommodation, food and drinks in a variety of places outside the home.

Hot holding: keeping cooked food hot so that it is ready to be served.

Hygiene Emergency Prohibition Notice: notice served if there is a serious risk of harm; it stops unsafe practices immediately.

Hygiene Improvement Notice: a notice that tells a business how to improve their food hygiene standards.

Internal organs: organ inside the human body, beneath the skin, for example the stomach, heart, lungs, and liver.

Kitchen brigade: the organisational hierarchy of staff in a professional kitchen.

Lactose: a sugar naturally found in milk.

Landfill site: a site where rubbish is buried in the ground.

Leach: to dissolve or drain off into a liquid.

Lifestyle: how someone chooses to live and spend their money.

Low biological value (LBV) proteins: proteins that lack one or more of the ten essential amino acids, for example nuts and lentils.

Mechanical equipment: equipment powered by humans.

Microbes: tiny micro-organisms, such as bacteria, yeasts and moulds, that can spoil food.

Mise en place: preparation before starting to cook.

Net profit: the amount of money made when all costs have been deducted.

Non-commercial establishment: a business that does not operate in order to make a profit.

Non-residential: a business that provides catering and hospitality services, but not accommodation.

Nutritional deficiency: eating too little food or too little of a nutrient to meet dietary needs.

Nutritional excess: eating too much food or too much of a nutrient.

Nutritional needs: which nutrients in particular an individual or group needs.

Onset time: the time it takes for the symptoms of food poisoning to appear after eating contaminated food.

Organoleptic: using the senses to assess the qualities of food.

Osteoporosis: a condition found in adults where a loss of calcium from bones makes them weak and more likely to break.

Out of order: not working correctly or not working at all.

PAT tested: all portable electrical appliances, including flexes and cables, need to be tested for safety by a qualified electrician.

Pathogenic: harmful; pathogenic bacteria can cause food poisoning.

Pellagra: a disease caused by a lack of vitamin B3; it causes inflammation of the skin, diarrhoea, fatigue and memory loss.

Personal attribute: a quality or characteristic of a person.

Personal protective equipment (PPE): clothing or equipment designed to protect people from harm.

Pest control: the regulation or management of a species defined as a pest, for example flies.

Pesticides: chemicals used to destroy insects or other organisms that could harm crops.

Portion size: the amount of food recommended for one person to eat in one sitting.

Poultry: the name given to birds that are reared for their meat and/or eggs, or both, such as chicken, duck, goose and turkey.

Preservation: treatment of food to prevent decay and to keep it safe for longer periods of time.

Pro rata: proportional/proportionally.

Recycled: converting waste products into reusable material.

Reference intake (RI): the maximum amount of calories/nutrients you should eat in a day.

Residential: a business that provides accommodation as well as catering and hospitality.

Rickets: a condition found in children where a lack of vitamin D and calcium in the diet causes the bones to soften.

Risk: how likely it is that someone could be harmed by a hazard.

Risk assessment: a way of identifying things that could cause harm to people in the workplace.

Salary: a fixed payment from an employer to an employee per pay period, for example monthly or annually.

Scurvy: an illness caused by a lack of vitamin C; it causes swollen, bleeding gums.

Seasonal foods: foods that are only available at certain times of the year.

Sequencing: preparing and cooking dishes in a suitable order so that the dishes are ready to serve on time.

Slicing: to cut a thin, broad piece from a large piece of food, or a wedge-shaped piece from a larger circular piece of food.

Sommelier: a specialist wine waiter.

Spore: dormant form of bacteria able to survive when conditions are not perfect, e.g. there is not enough water or the temperature is too hot or cold. When conditions improve, spores can produce more bacteria.

Starchy foods: foods that contain a large amount of starch, for example bread, rice, pasta and potatoes.

Starter culture: a small quantity of harmless bacteria that is used to start the fermentation of yoghurt or cheese.

Stock: all materials, ingredients and equipment used.

Sugary foods: foods that contain a large amount of refined sugar, for example biscuits, cakes and sweets.

Sustainable: doing something in a way that maintains and improves the environment for future generations.

Symptom: a sign or indication of an illness or disease.

Toque: a chef's hat.

Toxin: a poison, especially one produced by micro-organisms such as bacteria, yeasts and moulds.

Trend: the general direction in which something is changing.

Tronc: a fund in a hotel or restaurant into which tips and service charges are collected and then shared between staff.

Troncmaster: the person who collects and shares money in a tronc arrangement.

Use-by date: food must be consumed by this date to prevent food poisoning.

Variable costs: costs that change depending on the amount of business the establishment does, for example the amount of stock purchased.

VAT: a tax added to goods and services; the standard rate is currently 20 per cent.

Wage: money paid by an employer to an employee in exchange for work done; usually an hourly rate.

Water-soluble vitamins: vitamins that dissolve in water, for example the B group vitamins and vitamin C.

Well-balanced diet: a diet that contains all the nutrients in the correct amounts to meet individual needs.